Turbocharge Your Career on Your Lunch Hour

Maximizing Personal Development in Minimal Time

10 simple things you can do on your lunch hour that will Turbocharge your career!

By Dan Dyce CPCU RPA CTM

"I was fortunate to be a teammate of Dan early in both of our careers. Dan was different...a born leader who worked to understand the entire business, while becoming an expert in his assigned job. He took his career into his own hands and navigated a difficult industry to become completely successful. Read what he has to say and I promise you that you will pick up ideas that will put you in charge of your own career. A great read...quick...to the point and interesting. I highly recommend it."

—**Don Hurzeler, bestselling author, professional photographer and retired insurance company CEO, Kailua-Kona Hawaii**

"Turbocharge Your Lunch Hour is a game-changer that revolutionizes the way we perceive our lunch breaks. The book's insightful approach to maximizing career growth during these seemingly mundane hours is both refreshing and empowering. The author inspires readers to embark on an exciting journey of self-improvement. This is a must-read for anyone looking to make the most out of their workday."

—RDD, CEO Launchvox, Inc.
Granite Bay, California

"Time is our most valuable asset. In Turbocharge Your Career on Your Lunch Hour, Dan lays out a masterful plan of how to maximize your time and effort to advance your career. The personal examples bring the ideas to life. A must read for the young business professionals wanting to improve their career opportunities."

—Dr. John Burch, EdD College Professor
Camino, California

Turbo Publishing
Copyright © 2024 Dan Dyce
ISBN: 979-8-9900680-0-1

Dedication

To my wife, Sherryl, who I met when she was a senior in high school, and I was in my second year of college. She tells me that she quickly knew we would eventually get married. I had no clue.

We have now been married 53 years, and I can honestly say that marrying her was the best decision of my life. She was a stable partner as I bounced up and down the corporate ladder. We had two company transfers to different cities in order to retain my job, and she was a trouper all along the way. I was downsized (lost my job) at age 50 and was unemployed for nine months, she never lost faith.

Early in my career, she was a stay-at-home mom, which was a tremendous blessing in the overall development of two successful well-adjusted children. Having a stable home life with no drama is very helpful to being able to dedicate the time and effort it takes to keep and advance in a long-term career that is financially and personally rewarding. She got to go along on many of the adventures I talk about in this book. The fact that she was an English major in college also helped immensely in the final product you are reading right now.

Sweetheart, you are the love of my life, and you are responsible for much of whatever success I have achieved. You light up my life, and thanks for putting up with me!

Table of Contents

Introduction

Did you know that the average career person will spend about four years of their working life at lunch? No way? I can prove it!

Welcome to a journey of redefining your lunch hour, a time span we often disregard as insignificant. In this book, we challenge you to reconsider the ownership of this valuable time slot in your daily routine, and to inspire a shift in your thinking about how you use your lunch hour.

As we delve into the concept of the "lunch hour," it's important to note that it's not confined to a rigid 60-minute structure. Instead, it's a flexible period, encompassing the time it takes to nourish your body and the surplus time left over for personal endeavors. As the proprietor of your career, I will show you how to use some of these surplus hours to turbocharge your career.

Join us in this exploration of lunchtime possibilities. Embrace the possibility that this extra time can be transformed into moments of meaning, fulfillment, enjoyment, and even financial reward. This book serves as a collection of ideas, drawn from personal experiences and those of others who have turned their lunch hours into opportunities for growth and enrichment.

Your personal goal as you embark on this journey is to discover activities that add both joy and profit to your career. Ideas will be presented, and if you add a dash of your own motivation and self-discipline, you can transform some of your lunch hours into a time of excitement and accomplishment. While the transformation may not happen overnight, the long-term results will undoubtedly leave you astonished at what you can achieve.

"Don't wait for the opportunity; create it.
Proactivity is the key to career advancement."
— Anonymous

x

Chapter 1 –
Who Owns My Lunch Hour?

"Success is not just about climbing the ladder; it's about making the ladder work for you."
— Zig Ziglar

"Don't wait for the perfect moment; take the moment and make it perfect."
— Zoey Sayward, motivational speaker

The Premise of This Book

The premise of this book is that you can turbocharge your career by better utilizing your lunch hours. Therefore, the first order of business is to determine how much lunch hour time would be available to an average person during an average career.

- Assume you start working at age 25 and retire at age 65.
- This results in a 40-year work career.
- Let's use an average of eight work hours a day, plus a one-hour lunch. This amounts to a total of nine hours a day that you spend at your job.
- This means that 1/9th (11%) of every working day is spent at lunch. Let's call it 10% for the sake of easy math.
- Therefore, if 10% of each working day is spent at lunch, then over a 40-year career, you will have spent about four years at lunch. (10% of 40 years.)

Four years! Obviously, we can't pack all our lunch hours into one four-year block, so the goal is to carve out a portion of time from your "lunch hour" for meaningful activities that will further your career or at least make you a happier, more interesting person.

Let's start by rethinking who owns your lunch hour. Your body owns that part of your lunch hour that is necessary for eating your lunch and getting the nutrients that are necessary to give you the energy to accomplish your physical work tasks. Your mind owns any part of your lunch hour that is left over from the eating part of your lunch hour. You, as the owner of your career, own this extra lunch hour time and can do with it whatever you decide.

Your personal goal as you read this book is to find activities that you will do at lunch that add fun and profit to your life and career. I'll give you some ideas, and if you add some drive and self-discipline, you will find yourself embarking on an exciting new way to look at your lunch hours.

The Bureau of Labor Statistics studied how many jobs people hold in a lifetime. They did a long-term study that followed baby boomers through most of their careers. They concluded that many of us will experience multiple careers, with the average person holding around 11 jobs between the ages of 18 and 48. [www.edsurge.com › Search: "How many times will people change jobs"]

Knowing this is important, because it reminds us that any opportunity to acquire diverse skills that we don't currently use in our job may help us in our future roles. Also, skills such as writing and speaking are universally valuable, transcending specific job requirements.

Before we delve deeper into how to reclaim your lunch hour, it seems reasonable to understand what the law says about your lunch break. Interestingly, federal rules don't mandate lunch or other breaks for most employees, leaving it largely to state laws. Some states not only require breaks but also impose penalties for non-compliance. Knowing your rights empowers you to assert ownership of your lunch hour.

The Federal Law About Lunch Breaks

https://lunchbreaklaws.uslegal.com/federal-law-regarding-lunch-breaks/ "Under federal rules, employers do not need to give most employees lunch or other types of breaks at all. Lunch and meal breaks are largely a function of state law, which means different states have different rules. Some states not only require the employer to provide lunch and other breaks, but also imposes very specific penalties for failure to do so."

Each state has its own laws about lunch hours. For example, California law on this topic can be found at: http://lunchbreaklaws.uslegal.com/federal-law-regarding-lunch-breaks/

It reads in part: "You cannot employ someone for a work period of more than five hours without providing an unpaid, off-duty meal period of at least 30 minutes. The first meal period must be provided no later than the end of the employee's fifth hour of work. The employer satisfies its legal obligation to provide an off-duty meal period to its employees if it:

- Relieves its employees of all duty.
- Relinquishes control over their activities.

- Permits them a reasonable opportunity to take an uninterrupted, 30-minute break.
- Does not impede or discourage them from doing so.

It is very important that you do not let your boss make you feel guilty if you use your lunch hour for your own purposes instead of their work. I guarantee you that when you retire someday, you will not be wishing you had worked through more lunch hours.

Don't Steal From Your Employer

Maintaining honesty and integrity at work is fundamental, and a significant aspect of this commitment involves avoiding the misuse of your employer's time and resources for personal purposes. Simply put, when you don't devote the complete amount of time to your job that you're paid for, it's akin to stealing.

Consider this scenario: if your work contract specifies that you are expected to be present and engaged for eight hours a day, diverting any part of that time to personal matters would be inconsistent with the terms of your employment. This misuse of paid working hours not only violates the trust between you and your employer, but also diminishes the value of the compensation you receive for your professional services.

Utilizing your employer's photocopier for personal business is a breach of trust. Many photocopiers log usage, leaving a traceable electronic record. I vividly recall an incident at a previous workplace in which a colleague discreetly copied personal tax forms at the office. Despite his attempts at stealth, the electronic trail led to his discovery, resulting in probation. This incident not only impacted his reputation, but underscored the importance of maintaining honesty in professional conduct.

Similarly, using your company cell phone for personal matters is a form of misappropriation. It's important to remember that company resources, including electronic devices, are provided for work-related purposes. Misusing such resources can reflect negatively on your character, potentially jeopardizing your professional standing. Some companies allow personal calls on the company provided cell phone. Even in these cases, be careful because every call made on a cell phone leaves a footprint, and your company may have a right and probably can already see a list of every call you made and to whom it was made.

In essence, refraining from stealing from your employer goes beyond tangible items; it extends to the proper use of time, equipment, and resources. Upholding your commitment to honest and ethical conduct in the workplace is not only integral to maintaining a positive professional image, but also contributes to a culture of trust and integrity within the organization.

Your lunch hour is a precious part of your day, and it's important that you don't let your employer take it away from you. If you're currently stuck in the routine of working through lunch, breaking free from this habit becomes a more challenging initial step. You must firmly decide to stop doing it. It's likely that your boss expects you to work during lunch, and you might believe it's necessary to keep your job. However, you need to let your boss know that you can't continue with this practice. If she asks for a reason, you can show her this book as an example of why it's important to reclaim your lunch break. Stand your ground, be strong, and stick to your decision.

> **Stop right now and please agree with me that working through your lunch hour is not going to get you to your goal of turbocharging your career on your lunch hour.**

If you always work through lunch, some might label you a workaholic. While dedication and hard work are generally valued in the workplace, being a workaholic, which often implies an unhealthy and excessive obsession with work, may not necessarily guarantee promotion. Many organizations prioritize efficiency, productivity, and a healthy work-life balance.

Promotions often depend on a combination of factors, including:

1. Quality of Work: Consistently delivering high-quality work that aligns with the organization's goals.

2. Leadership Skills: Demonstrating leadership qualities, such as taking initiative, inspiring others, and effectively managing teams.

3. Collaboration: The ability to work well with others, contribute to a positive team culture, and communicate effectively.

4. Adaptability: Being open to change, learning new skills, and adapting to evolving work environments.

5. Problem-Solving: Showing the ability to identify and solve problems efficiently.

6. Networking: Building positive relationships within the organization and industry.

7. Strategic Thinking: Demonstrating an understanding of the bigger picture, and contributing to long-term organizational goals.

This book covers how you can demonstrate all of the above with some new creative lunchtime activities. Being a workaholic might lead to short-term gains, but it's essential to maintain a balance to prevent burnout and maintain overall well-being. Employers often value employees who can sustain high performance over the long term without sacrificing their health or personal life.

It's important to be aware of company culture and expectations, as well as to communicate with supervisors about career goals and expectations for advancement.

Let's start with an inventory of what you are currently doing for lunch. Are you munching at your desk, or grabbing some fast food and rushing back to work? By the time your bustling morning winds down, and noon rolls around, it might feel like the most efficient solution is to snag some pizza, a burger, fries, and a soda. Doing this takes up your whole lunch hour.

If you could bring lunch to work, it would save money and give you more free time at the end of your meal. Your time and money are valuable. The primary reason most people don't bring their own lunch is that they don't plan ahead. Imagine saving money and relishing a homemade, healthy, and delightful lunch. OK, this may be hard to imagine right now, but hang in here with me. Bringing your own lunch demands self-discipline and planning, and some of your coworkers might find it strange that you suddenly start bringing your own lunch to work. But I guarantee you that it pays off big in the long run. See Appendix A if you need some lunch ideas.

Beyond the potential financial savings, if you could initiate the habit of making and bringing your lunch, you wouldn't only save money but may also end up adopting a healthier eating routine. As a bonus, coupled with a bit of exercise, you could kickstart a gradual weight loss program.

Case Study: Emily's Lunch Makeover

Take Emily, for example, a working professional who used to grab fast food during her lunch break. One day, she decided to break the cycle and start bringing her own lunch. She invested a bit of time on Sundays, planning and preparing simple yet nutritious meals for the week.

Beyond the potential financial savings, Emily noticed a significant improvement in her overall well-being. Her energy levels soared, and she felt more focused in the afternoons. Additionally, she started shedding a few pounds over time, thanks to her healthier eating habits, and the newfound habit of incorporating a short walk into her lunch break.

Emily had to embrace a daily routine of assembling her lunch—a typical combo of a sandwich with lunchmeat and cheese on healthy bread, and an apple. She found contentment in this daily ritual, recognizing that lunch for her was no longer about a fancy dining experience and a social hour, but instead it became about sustenance and efficiency. Every week, during her household grocery shopping, she'd pick up some fresh bread, and some sliced meat and cheese from the deli counter at the grocery store.

Beyond the financial benefits of bringing her own lunch to work, the fact that Emily didn't have to go out to get lunch saved her time in her lunch hour. This time was then utilized for activities that turbocharged her afternoon productivity.

We all instinctively understand that a proper lunch significantly impacts our energy level for the afternoon, and who wouldn't want that? So, the key is not to skip lunch; instead, make it quick and easy so we can move on to more productive activities during our lunch hour.

The lazy, go along, get along, people in this world will take the path of least resistance. They feel that lunch is their free time to surf the net, check their social media, gab with their friends, etc. They are offended that I suggest they use part of their personal time for anything other than social activities. Don't hang out with those people, they will hold you back. You need to be different. It will feel awkward at first, but trust me, it feels a whole lot better to work at feeding your mind instead of feeding your ego. Be strong, you can do this. I did!

Now let's start looking at some more specific things you can do at lunch. The following chapters are in no particular order other than basic ideas for job skills come first, and the more fun, life enrichment ideas are at the end.

Choose Your Friends Wisely

Inc. magazine notes that: Warren Buffett has taught us many lessons appealing to our common sense. One of them was recently highlighted in Bill Gates's memorable 90th-birthday message to his close friend: "Of all the things I've learned from Warren," said Gates, "the most important thing might be what friendship is all about. As Warren himself put it a few years ago when we spoke with some college students, 'You will move in the direction of the people that you associate with.' So, it's important to associate with people that are better than yourself. The friends you have will form you as you go through life. Make some good friends, keep them for the rest of your life, but have them be people that you admire as well as like."

Motivational speaker Jim Rohn says that we are the average of the five people we spend the most time with. Jim Rohn's statement about being the average of the five people we spend the most time with encapsulates a profound concept that extends beyond mere social dynamics; it delves into the realm of personal development and the influence of our surroundings on our individual growth. This idea is closely tied to the law of averages, a statistical principle suggesting that the outcome of any situation tends to reflect the average of all possible outcomes.

In the context of personal development, the company we keep significantly shapes our beliefs, attitudes, and behaviors. Humans are inherently social beings, and we absorb the energy, values, and perspectives of those around us. Jim Rohn's insight encourages self-reflection on the impact of our social circles. If we surround ourselves with motivated, ambitious, and positive individuals, their qualities are likely to rub off on us. Conversely, spending time with negative, complacent, or uninspired people may hinder our personal growth.

The law of averages, in a broader sense, suggests that the collective influence of our social environment molds our individual experiences and outcomes. It acknowledges that life is a series of events, each influenced by a myriad of factors. By understanding this principle, we can recognize that our choices, behaviors, and achievements are often the culmination of various influences, including the people we associate with.

Applying these concepts in practical terms means actively choosing our social circles with intention. It involves surrounding ourselves with individuals who inspire, challenge, and uplift us. This process isn't about abandoning friends or family, but being mindful of the impact different relationships can have on our journey.

Moreover, the idea extends beyond just personal relationships to encompass broader aspects of life, such as work environments, communities, and even the content we consume. Being cognizant of the law of averages prompts us to seek environments that align with our aspirations and values.

In conclusion, Jim Rohn's statement serves as a powerful reminder of the interconnectedness between our social environment and personal development. Embracing the law of averages allows us to appreciate the cumulative effect of our choices and relationships on our overall life experiences. By consciously curating our social circles and surroundings, we can strive to become the best version of ourselves, driven by the positive influences that surround us.

Mike loves his job in technology, but he realized that the people he was hanging out with at lunch weren't very interested in learning new things. They were more into telling jokes and talking about last weekend or looking for next weekend's parties. So, Mike decided to find a tech meetup in his area.

> Meetup.com "Whatever your interest, from hiking and reading to networking and skill sharing, there are thousands of people who share it on Meetup. Events are happening every day — sign up to join the fun."

Mike found and attended a tech meetup at lunch in which he met a group of people who were passionate about coding and staying updated on the latest tech trends. Intrigued, Mike decided to spend more time with this new crew, and things began to change for him.

1. Positive Vibes:

    - Before: Mike's friends were not very enthusiastic about learning new tech stuff, and it made him feel a bit uninspired.

    - Transformation: Hanging out with his new tech-savvy friends got Mike excited about his job again. They shared cool tech discoveries, discussed new projects, and even collaborated on coding challenges.

- Outcome: Mike started feeling more motivated at work, and his renewed enthusiasm began to show in the quality of his projects.

2. Learning Together:

- Before: Mike often felt like he was on his own when it came to learning and staying updated on the latest in technology.

- Transformation: Joining his new group meant Mike had a bunch of buddies who shared his love for tech. They formed a study group, attended tech conferences together, and even worked on side projects.

- Outcome: Learning became more fun, and Mike found himself picking up new skills faster. The shared experiences expanded his knowledge and brought fresh ideas to his work.

3. Support System:

- Before: Mike felt a bit isolated in his passion for technology, with little en-couragement from his previous friends.

- Transformation: His new tech crew became a support system. They celebrated each other's career wins, offered advice during challenges at work, and even shared job opportunities.

- Outcome: Mike felt more connected and supported. The encouragement from his new friends helped him tackle work challenges with more confidence.

In summary, Mike's experience illustrates how the people we choose to be around can significantly impact our lives. By opting to spend time with friends who shared his passion for technology, Mike saw positive changes in his work life, learning journey, and overall happiness. This case study showcases the real-life application of the idea that we become the average of the people we spend the most time with.

Chapter 2 –
Networking is the Secret Sauce

"Invest in relationships; the currency of advancement is trust and collaboration."
— Arianna Huffington

"Alone we can do so little, together we can do so much."
— Helen Keller

Using Your Lunchtime to Network

If networking is the secret sauce, then lunchtime is the perfect place for purposeful networking. (Get it… lunch and sauce?) I use the term "networking" to mean any time spent getting to know and listening to other people. If you do an Internet search on "benefits of networking in the workplace," you get many pages of reasons why this is important and how to do it.

The purpose of networking is spending time with someone with the express purpose of getting to know them better, with an eye toward *what can I learn* that will help me in this or a future job?

The first bullet on this list is about sharing, not taking. If your networking efforts come off as *what can you do for me*, that person will not give you much time now or in the future. But if you have a genuine interest in getting to know that person, and sharing anything that can help them, then you will benefit in the long run.

When you go to lunch with someone with the express purpose of networking, you need to listen twice as much as you talk. If you are a talker, and you just want to go to lunch to tell them all about yourself, then don't bother. You will be killing your network rather than expanding it.

> **Here are some of the key networking benefits:**
> - Strengthen business connections, networking is about sharing, not taking
> - Get fresh ideas
> - Advance your career
> - Get access to job opportunities
> - Interconnected business contacts = more knowledge
> - Get career advice and support
> - Build confidence
> - Gain a different perspective
>
> www.michaelpage.com.au>advice>career-progression (Nov. 5, 2018)

Very Important Rule of Conversation!

Remember this very important rule of conversation. When someone asks you about something, that is code for *I want to tell you about that something.* For example, if someone starts a conversation with "Have you been anyplace fun lately?" They really want to tell you about something fun that they have done recently. So, give them a short answer, or no answer, and turn it back to them with a "What about you, have you been anyplace fun lately?" And sit back and let them talk. And then while they talk, <u>do not interrupt</u>!

I am especially annoyed by people who always want to be part of a group conversation but don't have anything relevant to say. They feel like they need to have an opinion or contribute because they just like to talk. I call these people "over-talkers." As soon as someone mentions something like, I really enjoyed my trip to Niagara Falls last summer, over-talkers feel the need to tell me about a cousin or friend of a friend who always wanted to go to Niagara Falls but never made it, or some other uninteresting comment that adds nothing meaningful to the conversation. Please, do not be an "over-talker!" Some of you do this and don't know that you do this. Even if you think this is not you, right now I want you to copy this paragraph and send it to several friends, and ask them for their honest opinion whether this is an area you can improve on. If you feel that others sometimes don't include you in conversations, this may be the reason. Better to nip this bad habit now before you further isolate yourself.

Your email on this topic could go something like this:

Hi John,

I am reading a book and one of my assignments is to copy a paragraph in the book and send it to a couple of friends. Here is the paragraph: "I am especially annoyed by people who always want to be part of a group conversation, but don't have anything relevant to say. They feel like they need to have an opinion or contribute because they just like to talk. I call these people "over-talkers." As soon as someone mentions something like, I really enjoyed my trip to Niagara Falls last summer, over-talkers feel the need to tell me about a cousin or friend of a friend who always wanted to go to Niagara Falls but never made it, or some other uninteresting comment that adds nothing meaningful to the conversation. Please, do not be an "over-talker!" Some of you do this and don't know that you do this. Even if you think this is not you, right now I want you to copy this paragraph and send it to several friends, and ask them for their honest opinion whether this is an area you can improve on. If you feel that others sometimes don't include you in conversations, this may be the reason. Better to nip this bad habit now, before you further isolate yourself."

John, I don't know if this is me, but I need to complete this assignment so if this is even a little bit me, please be honest and tell me.

Thanks!

People Love Listeners

People need listeners. So be a good listener, and people will love you! Be a "talk too much person" or an "over-talker" and people will find ways to avoid you.

During my career, I purposely invited co-workers, people in other departments, my boss, my subordinates, and other people in my industry to go out to lunch with me on a regular basis. This was purposeful networking by me. This takes a little planning and scheduling. And sometimes if I was in the lunchroom eating the lunch I brought from home, I asked people I did not know well if I could join them.

When you do get the opportunity to spend quality time with someone, remember these points: Make it enjoyable, be purposeful, ask lots of questions, listen more than you talk. This is not a gab fest. In the end, you will learn a lot about them. They will probably learn very little about you, but I guarantee you, they will think you were terrific company!

I once heard from one of my network contacts about a position at a company that planned to hire someone several months in the future. I called the company, and they told me they did not have an opening right now but wanted to talk to me anyway. I went and met with the manager of that team, and he did all the talking. I didn't care, I just wanted the job. But it felt weird to sit there and let him tell me all about the job and the company, and not really dig into my past and skills. To be fair, he had heard about me from an industry friend, so he probably knew more about me than I thought. Maybe he felt he needed to sell me on the job and company. Several months later, I was offered the job.

This example also proves the axiom (Axiom – a statement that is regarded as being established, accepted, or self-evidently true) that lots of good jobs never get advertised, but rather are filled by referrals. Further validating the need for a good network of industry friends who are looking out for you.

Here is another example of the benefits of my previous networking efforts. I was at a luncheon meeting for people who worked in my industry (property insurance claims). One of the guys at my table was bemoaning the fact that his office manager / assistant was leaving, and he hated the idea of advertising for, then finding, then training a new person for the job. Most of the people at the table were commiserating and telling stories about when they had gone through similar circumstances.

I on the other hand started asking questions about what skills he was looking for. I learned that he had a small four-person office, with three accountants, and one office manager / assistant who did everything from answering phone calls, to keeping the office photocopy paper ordered, to completing complex spreadsheets. I learned that he wanted a mature person, who wouldn't be calling in sick all the time. He needed someone who was good with computer spreadsheets as well as customer service. Since it was a small office, and he and his staff were sometimes out of the office, he needed someone who was a self-starter and could work independently. I told him I had someone in mind who might fit his needs.

You can tell by my questions that I was purposefully networking. This is because my wife had recently shared with me that she was not happy with her current job situation. I knew what my wife liked to do, what she was good at, and the kind of job environment she preferred. I went home and told her about the position, and she agreed to check it out and learn more about the opportunity. The end of this story is that she got the position, and to this day agrees that it was the right job for her at that stage in her life. She worked there for eight years until she retired. One bonus for me, beyond having a happy wife, is that this office was part of a much larger chain of offices, and they threw great Christmas parties every year that I got to attend as an employee's spouse.

Again, proving the axiom that lots of good jobs never get advertised, but rather are filled by referrals.

Networking When Looking for a Job

After 19 years with my company, they were closing the office where I worked, and to continue my employment with that company I would have to move to another city and state. My wife was not happy about that, and my kids were ready to boycott Dad, if he made them move into new schools and make new friends. So, I immediately started contacting my industry network to see if anyone knew of job opportunities for a person with my experience and qualifications.

I would not have been able to call on these individuals if I had not previously, over many lunches, built up this network of business acquaintances. I established this network over many previous years before I ever knew that I might someday need to call on them about job opportunities. The point is, you can't start networking when you need something from a network. And you don't build a network with the idea of what it can do for you. You build a network by having a bunch of fun interactions with different individuals over several years. You learn from your network, you share with your network, you nurture your network, and when you ever need something from your network, hopefully you have built up enough goodwill so that the network might be useful to you. If I had been an "over-talker" that no one wanted to be around, my network would have been very slim. But because I am the type of person who is genuinely interested in others, I have a very large network.

As I was working my way through my network contacts, my question for them was NOT *do you have a job for me*, but *do you KNOW anyone who might need a guy with my skills and experience*? The happy ending to this networking story is that one of my contacts had heard about a company that was looking for a guy like me. It took me six months to finally land that job, but it turned out to be a better paying and more secure position than the one I was leaving. This new job was never advertised, further proving the axiom that lots of good jobs never get advertised, but rather are filled by referrals.

Here are some tips to help you foster and maintain strong professional connections:

1. Effective Communication:

    - Be clear and concise in your communication.

    - Listen actively to others, and show genuine interest in what they have to say. Don't be an over-talker!

    - Respond promptly to emails and messages.

2. Industry Networking:

    - Attend industry events, conferences, and seminars to meet professionals in your field.

    - Utilize online platforms like LinkedIn to connect with colleagues, peers, and mentors.

    - Join professional organizations relevant to your industry.

3. Build Trust:

    - Be reliable and fulfill your commitments.

    - Demonstrate integrity and honesty in your actions.

    - Avoid gossip and negative talk about others.

4. Show Appreciation:

    - Acknowledge the contributions of your colleagues and express gratitude.

    - Give credit where it's due, and celebrate the success of others.

    - Small gestures, such as a thank-you note, can go a long way.

5. Be Genuine and Authentic:

    - Be yourself; authenticity builds trust.

    - Share your experiences–both successes, and failures.

    - People are more likely to connect with you if they perceive you as genuine.

6. Help Others:

    - Offer assistance when colleagues need help.

    - Share your knowledge and expertise.

    - Actively contribute to the success of your team and colleagues.

7. Maintain a Positive Attitude:

    - Stay positive, even in challenging situations.

    - Be a problem solver, and contribute to a positive work environment.

    - Positivity is contagious and can enhance relationships.

8. Stay Professional:

    - Maintain a professional demeanor in both in-person and online interactions.

    - Be mindful of your language and behavior.

    - Respect boundaries, and treat everyone with courtesy.

9. Socialize Outside of Work:

    - Participate in social events organized by your workplace.

    - Grab coffee or lunch with colleagues.

    - Building personal connections can strengthen professional relationships.

    - When I worked in Denver, Colorado, they were big on bowling, so I joined the company bowling league. I got to hang out with people from other departments, and build cordial relationships that carried over into my work interactions.

10. Adaptability:

    - Be open to new ideas and ways of working.

    - Adapt to changes in the workplace and industry.

    - Flexibility and adaptability are valuable traits in professional relationships.

Remember, building lasting professional relationships takes time and effort. Consistency in your actions, and a genuine interest in others will contribute to the strength and longevity of these connections.

Consider Lunchtime Meetups

Lunchtime meetups refer to informal gatherings or events that take place during the lunch hours, in which individuals come together to network, share ideas, and socialize. These meetups are often organized around a specific theme, industry, or interest, and are designed to provide participants with an opportunity to connect with like-minded individuals in a casual setting. Making the most of local lunchtime meetups can have several benefits:

1. Networking Opportunities:

    - Lunchtime meetups provide a platform for professionals, entrepreneurs, and enthusiasts to expand their network. Building connections with people in your local community can lead to potential collaborations, partnerships, or job opportunities.

2. Knowledge Sharing:

    - These events often feature discussions, presentations, or workshops related to a specific topic or industry. Attending these meetups can enhance your knowledge and provide insights into the latest trends and developments in your field.

3. Community Building:

    •   Lunchtime meetups contribute to the development of a sense of community among local individuals who share common interests. This sense of community fosters collaboration and support among members.

4. Skill Development:

    •   Workshops or skill-sharing sessions that are a part of lunchtime meetups can help individuals enhance their skills. Whether it's learning about a new technology, industry best practices, or soft skills, these events can contribute to personal and professional growth.

5. Stay Informed:

    •   Local meetups are an excellent way to stay informed about what's happening in your industry or community. You might learn about upcoming events, job opportunities, or changes in the local business landscape.

6. Socializing and Team Building:

    •   Lunchtime meetups provide a more relaxed and social atmosphere, compared to formal networking events. This can make it easier for participants to connect on a personal level, fostering relationships that extend beyond professional interactions.

7.   Break from Routine:

- Attending lunchtime meetups can provide a welcome break from the daily work routine. It allows individuals to step outside their usual environment, meet new people, and gain a fresh perspective on their work and interests.

To make the most of local lunchtime meetups, consider the following tips:

1.   Research Events:

- Stay informed about upcoming meetups in your area by joining relevant online communities, subscribing to newsletters, or using event platforms.

2.   Set Goals:

- Determine what you want to achieve from each meetup, whether it's expanding your network, learning a new skill, or finding potential collaborators.

3.   Be Open-Minded:

- Approach these meetups with an open mind. Be willing to engage with people from diverse backgrounds and industries.

4. Bring Business Cards:

    *   If appropriate, bring business cards to share your contact information with others. If your company does not provide them, get your own made up. They are an inexpensive way to add to your professional image. Obviously you may not be able to use your company's name or logo, but make up a personal card for you. At one point I made up cards that said "Free Agent." I was unemployed at the time and looking for a job.

5. Participate Actively:

    *   Engage in discussions, ask questions, and participate in any activities or workshops offered during the meetup.

6. Follow Up:

    *   After the meetup, follow up with individuals you connected with. This could be through email, LinkedIn, or other professional networking platforms.

By actively participating in local lunchtime meetups, you can leverage these opportunities to enhance both your personal and professional life.

Online Networking – A New Frontier

Online networking refers to the practice of connecting and interacting with others over the internet to exchange information, ideas, and resources. It involves using various online platforms, and tools to establish and maintain professional or personal relationships. Online networking has become increasingly important in the digital age, providing opportunities for communication, collaboration, and community-building.

Some common forms of online networking include:

1. Social Media Networking: Platforms like Facebook, Twitter, LinkedIn, and Instagram enable users to create profiles, connect with others, and share content. These platforms are widely used for both personal and professional networking.

2. Professional Networking: Websites like LinkedIn are specifically designed for professional networking. Users can create detailed profiles, connect with colleagues and professionals in their industry, join groups, and participate in discussions.

3. Forums and Communities: Online forums and community platforms, such as Reddit, Quora, or specialized forums related to specific industries or interests, provide spaces for users to ask questions, share

knowledge, and connect with like-minded individuals.

4. Online Conferences and Events: With the rise of virtual events, professionals can attend conferences, webinars, and workshops from the comfort of their homes. These events often include networking opportunities through virtual booths, chat rooms, and video meetings.

5. Blogging and Content Sharing: Blogging platforms like WordPress, Medium, or personal websites allow individuals to share their expertise, thoughts, and experiences. This can attract a network of readers and followers.

6. Collaborative Platforms: Tools like Slack, Microsoft Teams, and other collaboration platforms facilitate communication and project collaboration among teams, fostering networking within organizations.

7. Online Learning Platforms: Educational platforms, like Coursera, edX, or Udacity not only offer courses but also provide opportunities for networking with other learners, instructors, and professionals in the field.

Effective online networking involves creating a compelling online presence, engaging with others in a meaningful way, and leveraging the available tools to build and maintain relationships. It can be a valuable resource for career development, learning, and staying connected in an increasingly digital world.

Earlier I wrote about how my network helped me find a new job. Have you heard the saying?

If You Want to be One, You Need to Look Like One

Do you want to climb the career ladder at your current job? Well, the concept of "dressing for your next job" becomes even more crucial in that scenario. It's not just about clothes; it's about signaling to your bosses and colleagues that you're ready for a promotion and eager to take on more responsibilities. Consider this: you're in an office job, and your goal is to become a manager. Dressing for your next job means wearing the attire of a manager, even if you haven't quite reached that role yet. Trade in your everyday jeans for some sharp, professional pants, and swap that casual shirt for something a bit more polished.

By doing so, you're not just changing your outfit; you're transforming the way others perceive you within the workplace. It's like sending a visual message that says, "I'm not just content where I am; I'm ready for the next level." This shift in appearance communicates ambition and dedication, showcasing your commitment to personal and professional growth. Your attire becomes a silent statement that aligns with your career goals.

Moreover, dressing for the position you aspire to is more than what you wear—it's about embodying the qualities and characteristics of that role. So, beyond the attire, it involves adopting a mindset and work ethic that mirrors the expectations of the desired position. When you dress and carry yourself like someone in a higher role, it not only influences how others perceive you, but also has an effect on how you see yourself. This positive mindset can translate into increased confidence, boosting your chances of getting noticed for promotions and additional opportunities.

Imagine you want a cool job in a big tech company, but you're currently working in a different place. Dressing for your next job means wearing clothes that match the style of the job you want, not the one you have right now. So, if you dream of being a tech wizard, maybe swap the casual look for something a bit more tech-savvy. It's like sending a message with your clothes that says, "I'm ready for the next big thing!" Dressing the part helps people see your potential, and shows you're serious about where you want to go in your career.

In essence, the idea of dressing for your next job is a holistic approach to career advancement. It's about aligning your external presentation with your internal aspirations, creating a harmonious narrative that speaks volumes about your readiness for growth. So, go ahead, make that shift in your wardrobe, and watch how it becomes a catalyst for your journey up the professional ladder.

Speaking of the appropriate attire for the job, I want to share a bit of creative advice. I was invited to attend a conference in our home office in Philadelphia, Pennsylvania. My boss said he would meet me at the airport for our Sunday morning flight to Pennsylvania. He said there would be a Sunday evening reception at our hotel followed by two days of meetings in the home office building. I asked him what the dress code for the meetings was, and he informed me it would be business casual.

I showed up at the airport in my finest business casual attire, which was a nice pair of brown slacks, a white polo shirt, topped by a very stylish 1980s brown corduroy jacket with very wide lapels. My boss showed up at the airport in a suit and tie. "Hey boss, what gives, you told me that the dress code was business casual, why are you dressed in a suit and tie?" He informed me that "the meeting next week is business casual, but the Sunday evening reception that we are having with the CEO of the company tonight is formal." Dang!

I was not happy because I had not packed a suit or a tie, so what to do? I thought maybe when I got to the Philadelphia airport, I could buy a tie in one of those airport shops, although I knew it would be expensive, and we didn't have the time to go shopping. As we were flying back East, I noticed that the male United flight attendant was sporting a very nice blue and red striped tie with United logos all over it. I explained my problem and asked the attendant if I could buy his tie. He said he could not sell his tie to me, but if I would wait and be the last one off the plane, he would give it to me. All he wanted in exchange was for me to fill out a feedback form about the great in-flight service he had provided to us on our flight.

Perfect, I filled out the form, and he gave me his tie as I walked off the plane. There were about 50 of us at the reception that evening, all wearing professional attire, and I showed up with the non-matching United logo tie on my polo shirt and stylish brown corduroy jacket. I hoped that I could hang out in the sidelines and hopefully my career was not over. But my boss told someone the story about how I was able to talk a flight attendant out of a tie. And next thing I know, the CEO wants to meet the clever fellow who is wearing the United logo tie. The bottom line is sometimes stuff happens that is out of your control. You must develop the self-confidence to make the best of it and don't apologize, just go with the flow. I would not have gotten to spend quality time with the CEO if that had not happened.

In 1915, American writer Elbert Hubbard coined the phrase "When life gives you lemons, make lemonade!" That is what I did, and it turns out to be a good motto to follow!

Chapter 3 – Earn a Degree or a Professional Designation

"Learn as if you will live forever, work as if you will die tomorrow. Continuous learning propels career growth." — Mahatma Gandhi

"Your brand is what people say about you when you're not in the room. Build a reputation that opens doors." — Jeff Bezos

Are you a few credits short of completing your college degree? Perhaps you're contemplating the acquisition of an industry-specific license or certificate to bolster your career prospects. Well, here's a practical suggestion: consider utilizing a portion of your lunch breaks to make headway on these educational aspirations. It's an effective strategy to gradually chip away at your goals. The key ingredient here is time; during lunch periods, you often have a window of opportunity that, with a dash of self-discipline and motivation, can be dedicated to advancing your education.

Completing Your Degree

Take the scenario in which you're on the brink of completing your degree, but a few elective courses remain. Using your lunch break to enroll and study for these courses not only allows you to make steady progress, but also demonstrates your commitment to continuous learning.

There are numerous online colleges and universities that offer flexible programs to help individuals complete their college degrees. Keep in mind that the availability of programs may vary, based on your location and the specific degree you are pursuing. Also, there are cost considerations. Hopefully where you work has a plan to financially help employees who take the initiative to complete a degree. Here are some well-known and reputable online institutions that you might consider:

1. Southern New Hampshire University (SNHU): SNHU is a private, nonprofit university known for its extensive online degree programs. They offer a variety of undergraduate and graduate programs in fields such as business, healthcare, education, and more.

2. University of Maryland Global Campus (UMGC): UMGC specializes in providing online education for adult learners. They offer a range of undergraduate and graduate programs, particularly in areas like cybersecurity, business, and education.

3. Arizona State University Online (ASU Online): ASU Online is the online platform of Arizona State University, offering a diverse range of programs at the undergraduate and graduate levels. ASU is known for its innovative and high-quality online education.

4. Western Governors University (WGU): WGU is a nonprofit, competency-based university that offers online degree programs in areas such as business, education, information technology, and healthcare.

5. Penn State World Campus: Penn State's World Campus provides a variety of online degree programs, including bachelor's and master's degrees, in fields such as business, engineering, health, and more.

6. Liberty University Online: Liberty University is a private Christian university offering a wide range of online programs at various degree levels. They cover diverse fields such as business, education, psychology, and theology.

7. University of Florida Online: UF Online offers a selection of bachelor's degree programs in areas like business administration, computer science, and public relations. It is an extension of the University of Florida.

8. Colorado State University Global Campus: CSU Global Campus is an online university affiliated with the Colorado State University system. They offer a variety of undergraduate and graduate programs in fields such as business management and information technology.

Before enrolling in any online program, it's crucial to research each institution thoroughly, ensuring that it is accredited and recognized for the specific program you are interested in. Accreditation is a key factor in determining the legitimacy and quality of an online degree program. Additionally, consider factors such as tuition costs, course structure, and support services to find the program that best fits your needs and goals.

Earn an Industry-Specific Certificate

Similarly, if there's a valuable industry-specific certification that could propel your career, investing lunchtime hours in preparing for and obtaining that certification becomes a very smart strategic move.

Now, let's delve into a case study to illustrate how this approach can yield tangible benefits. Meet Alex, an aspiring marketing professional working a full-time job. Despite being on the cusp of completing a marketing degree, Alex felt the need to enhance practical skills to stand out in the competitive job market. During lunch breaks, Alex enrolled in an online course that focused on the latest digital marketing trends and strategies.

The small, consistent effort made during lunch breaks allowed Alex to grasp new concepts without overwhelming the existing workload. This initiative not only expanded Alex's knowledge, but also boosted his confidence. Eventually, armed with the additional skills acquired during those lunchtime learning sessions, Alex secured a promotion within the company, transitioning into a role with more responsibilities and opportunities for growth.

In essence, the lunchtime learning approach emphasizes the transformative power of taking small, intentional steps toward educational and career goals. By signing up for that course or class during lunch breaks, you lay the foundation for meaningful progress and future success. It's a testament to the idea that, sometimes, the journey to achievement begins with a simple commitment to invest time wisely during those midday breaks.

My first real career job was with Allstate Insurance Company in Pasadena, California. I was 24 years old and had just graduated from college with a business degree. Prior to graduation, I had no idea what I wanted to be when I grew up, so I chose a business major with the idea that I wanted to be in management with a big company where I could work 8 to 5 and not work on weekends. Not a lofty goal, but a clear path forward.

After I graduated, I went to my college placement center, which sent me out on job interviews with large companies that were looking for entry-level management trainees. I was interviewed by retail stores and financial service companies. Retail involved working at stores that were open nights and weekends. I ended up taking a job with Allstate Insurance Company, because it was an office environment, and their offices were closed on nights and weekends. After some training, I was assigned as the supervisor of a customer service unit. All day long, my team of five and I took calls from Allstate customers and Allstate insurance agents. Very few called to tell us how great we were doing. Most had a question that we would answer, or a problem that we would help solve. I became good at knowing the technical information that I needed to do that specific job. But I was working in the insurance industry, and

I knew very little about this industry. It was clear that to advance at this company, or to be attractive to another company, I needed knowledge beyond what I could learn on this job.

I happened onto our company benefit materials and learned that Allstate would pay for employees to take a training course that required passing 10 extensive exams. It was equivalent to earning a master's degree in insurance. When you passed all 10 exams, you were given the designation of CPCU. This stands for Chartered Property and Casualty Underwriter. A fancy title that means you have learned a lot about how the entire insurance industry works. It looked like a five-year commitment, but I knew that I had a lot of boring lunch hours in which I could study the material for the exams. A CPCU was way more than I needed to know to do my current job, but I could tell it carried a lot of prestige in the company and the insurance industry.

How I Used my Lunch Hour for a Trip to Hawaii

I also learned that as an incentive to earn a CPCU, Allstate would send me and my significant other (in my case a spouse) to the national convention, plus give you a $500 bonus. I looked at the chart of national CPCU convention locations, and saw that in five years the convention was to be held in Hawaii. I went home that night and told my wife that I was taking her to Hawaii in five years. This was a big deal for a young man who was making a very modest income at that time.

Promising to take her to Hawaii was the easy part. Planning to study and pass those exams took dedication and perseverance. Any task can be accomplished if you break it down into small actions. Step one for me was to sign up for the first class. Step two was to dedicate a small part of a whole bunch of lunch hours to studying the material, instead of going to the cafeteria and gabbing with my co-workers. Step 3 was to sign up for the exams. This gave me a target date that I knew I had to be ready for. It is easy not to sign up, to not take that first step, but that first small step is what starts moving you towards that distant finish line.

The end of this story is that I passed all my exams. Yes, it took me five years to complete all the course work, but in 1980 I took my wife to Hawaii where I received my CPCU designation, and the company paid for everything; airfare, hotel, food, the works!

But... that is not the end of my CPCU story. I was working in Los Angeles at the time, and now that I had become a CPCU, I was invited to join the Los Angeles chapter of the CPCU Society. The CPCU Society held a monthly luncheon meeting for which they brought in industry speakers. We sat at round tables for the presentations, which gave me a perfect opportunity to meet and network with other professionals from my industry. Allstate supported their employees with CPCU designations attending these luncheons; they allowed for the extra time these lunch meetings took; and they reimbursed me for the cost of these lunch meetings. Free lunches were always a high priority for me. Now I was getting to know people from outside my company. The point being when you think of your networking opportunities, think inside your company as well as outside your company.

Get Involved With a Professional Organization

Getting involved with professional organizations within your industry can be a strategic and beneficial step for career growth and personal development. These organizations provide a platform for networking, learning, and staying updated on industry trends. Consider the following reasons why it's important to engage with professional organizations in your industry:

1. Networking Opportunities: Professional organizations offer a unique space for networking with individuals from diverse backgrounds, companies, and roles within your industry. Connecting with professionals outside your current workplace expands your professional circle, potentially opening doors to new opportunities, collaborations, and partnerships.

2. Knowledge Sharing and Learning: Being part of a professional organization provides

access to a wealth of industry knowledge. Members often share insights, best practices, and the latest developments through conferences, seminars, webinars, and publications. This exposure can enhance your understanding of industry trends and advancements.

3. Career Development: Professional organizations frequently offer resources for career development, including workshops, mentorship programs, and career fairs. Engaging with these opportunities can help you acquire new skills, receive guidance from experienced professionals, and explore potential career paths.

4. Visibility and Recognition: Active participation in professional organizations can enhance your visibility within your industry. Involvement in committees, presenting at conferences, or contributing to publications can position you as a thought leader and contribute to professional recognition.

5. Access to Job Opportunities: Many professional organizations have job boards, newsletters, or online platforms where members can find job opportunities within the industry. This can be particularly beneficial when you are seeking new challenges or considering a career change.

6. Professional Development and Training: These organizations often provide opportunities for continuous learning and skill development. Whether through webinars, workshops, or certifications, you can stay current with industry standards and improve your professional competencies.

7. Industry Advocacy and Influence: Professional organizations often play a role in advocating for industry interests and influencing policy decisions. By being an active member, you contribute to the collective voice of the industry and can stay informed about developments that may impact your profession.

8. Diverse Perspectives: Interacting with professionals from various companies and backgrounds exposes you to diverse perspectives and approaches to problem-solving. This can broaden your understanding of the industry and stimulate innovative thinking.

In summary, getting involved with professional organizations is not just about meeting people outside your current workplace; it's a strategic investment in your professional growth. By actively participating in these communities, you gain access to a wide range of resources, opportunities, and connections that can contribute significantly to your career advancement and overall success in your industry.

Back to my CPCU story. I was now working in Sacramento, California, and the Sacramento CPCU Society had a board of directors that was made up of five chairs. Board members started at the bottom chair and worked their way through the five chairs, advancing every year until they were President. The chairs were: Public Relations Director, Education Director, Secretary, Vice President, President. At one of these luncheon meetings, I learned that our chapter sent their President and significant other to the annual national CPCU convention. I was a new CPCU, and all the people that I saw on the board of directors looked like older, long-term industry icons to me. I couldn't even imagine what it would take to eventually get on that board of directors.

When I showed up at the next monthly luncheon meeting, they were taking nominations for next year's Public Relations (PR) Director, who would in five years eventually be the chapter president. It turns out that most people don't want to be on the board of directors, because it requires extra meetings and work, and putting yourself out there in front of your industry peers. So, the chapter was having trouble getting a nomination for the PR Director position. I told my table mates that I was fairly new, but if they wanted to nominate me, I would give it a shot. After which someone promptly stood up and nominated me for the PR board position. Then they closed the nominations, and I was unanimously voted in as the new PR Chairperson for the Sacramento Chapter of the CPCU Society. I had dressed for success, and I looked like I could do it, even though I had a very limited idea of what I was getting into. But, I knew that hanging out with the other board members would be a great way to meet and network with other high-caliber industry professionals.

Have you heard the term "fake it until you make it?" This is a popular saying that suggests acting as if you are already successful or accomplished, even if you haven't reached that level yet. The idea behind this concept is to project confidence, competence, and a positive image, with the belief that doing so can lead to actual success or achievement over time. While this approach can have its merits, it's important to approach it with caution and nuance. While projecting confidence and adopting a positive mindset can be beneficial, it's crucial to balance this with authenticity, competence, and ethical behavior. "Faking it until you make it" should not be an excuse to deceive or compromise your values; rather, it should be a tool for personal and professional development. In the case of me putting myself out there for this board position, it didn't involve much risk, because I knew if I got the position, there were people who would teach me what I needed to know to be successful.

At our first CPCU board meeting, which was during lunch, and for which my company reimbursed me, they gave me a manual detailing everything that the public relations director's position was required to do. When I volunteered, I didn't even know they had a manual detailing my new responsibilities. Following is a summary of what it contained. I bet that after you read the requirements, you will agree that you could do this job as well. It was not about what I knew or the experience I had, it was about me having the guts to step out and figure it out as you go. Here is what the CPCU PR Director's duties were:

"Public Relations is responsible for enhancing the image of the CPCU Chapter, its members and the CPCU Society. Among its activities are the publication of a chapter newsletter, distribution of press releases, distribution of public service announcements, and advertising." Piece of cake, right?

It turned out to be a fun job, which included writing articles about our CPCU chapter for industry newsletters. It also allowed me to network with others from my industry who were not from the company where I worked. This networking opportunity would not have happened if I had not been willing to take a chance on joining that board of directors. I loved seeing my name in print for the articles I researched and wrote, and the fact that I got published helped me later in my career.

At a later board meeting, I learned that the CPCU Annual Convention would be in Hawaii in exactly five years after I joined the board, which meant that the convention would be in Hawaii the year I was president of the CPCU board. I went home that night and told my wife; "I am taking you to Hawaii again in five years." She is a patient woman.

Now, here is an interesting wrinkle to my CPCU board of directors' story that has nothing to do with networking or turbocharging your career. During my third year in the chairs, the guy ahead of me got transferred out of town by his company, which meant everyone moved up one chair. That meant if I moved up one board chair, I would be going to San Francisco when I was president instead of Hawaii. I was living in Sacramento, California, at that time, and San Francisco was a two-hour drive for me, and a place I had been many times. So, I negotiated with the lady behind me to jump over me, and she went to San Francisco, and my wife and I went to Hawaii during my fifth year as president of the Sacramento CPCU board of directors.

Beyond everything I learned and all the fun I had was the fact that at every one of those lunch board meetings, I was building up my network of people who I genuinely liked, and who liked and cared about me.

The bottom line for you, the reader, is that you must figure out your own opportunities and path, but get involved, get on committees, get on governing boards if you can, and find ways to build your network!

Chapter 4 -
Improve Your Public
Speaking Skills

"Mastering the art of public speaking isn't just about conveying information; it's about empowering others through the transformative magic of your words." — Anonymous

"Embrace feedback as the breakfast of champions. Constructive criticism is your guide to improvement." — Ken Blanchard

Fear of Public Speaking

The fear of public speaking is the most common phobia ahead of death, spiders, or heights. The National Institute of Mental Health reports that "public speaking anxiety, or glossophobia, affects about 73% of the population."

One of the top skills of any person in their field of work is communication skills. A great way to improve speaking skills is to join a lunchtime Toastmasters club. About five years into my career, I realized that successful people in my industry were good public speakers. So, I set about finding a way to improve my speaking skills, and I ran across Toastmasters.

What I learned is that my local Toastmasters club met at lunchtime. Perfect! This sounded like something that would be a worthwhile use of an occasional lunch hour. I talked to my boss and found out that our human resource department (AKA Personnel) liked employees to join Toastmasters, and would pay for the Toastmaster dues, including the cost of the monthly luncheons. Wow, another free lunch!

So, I joined Toastmasters and received a manual that laid out 10 speeches that needed to be completed to earn a CTM (Competent Toastmaster) designation. That sounded good to me, so over the next year, I completed the 10 speeches. Now I can use the CTM designation after my name – see the front cover.

Here is a list of the first 10 speeches. Each is five- to seven-minutes long.

- Speech #1: The Ice Breaker
- Speech #2: Organize Your Speech
- Speech #3: Get To the Point
- Speech #4: How To Say It
- Speech #5: Your Body Speaks
- Speech #6: Vocal Variety
- Speech #7: Research Your Topic
- Speech #8: Get Comfortable With Visual Aids
- Speech #9: Persuade With Power
- Speech #10: Inspire Your Audience

The club meetings are fun, and you give your 10 speeches to your club. The club members give you feedback after every speech. And there is the "AH" bell. Every time you hesitate or say Ah, or Umm, etc., someone would ring a bell which quickly broke you of that annoying speaking habit. This was another opportunity to network, and get to know some interesting people from outside my industry.

The Toastmasters Website reads: "Toastmasters International is a nonprofit educational organization that builds confidence and teaches public speaking skills through a worldwide network of clubs that meet online and in person. In a supportive community or corporate environment, members prepare and deliver speeches, respond to impromptu questions, and give and receive constructive feedback. It is through this regular practice that members are empowered to meet personal and professional communication goals. Founded in 1924, the organization is head-quartered in Englewood, Colorado, with approximately 270,000 members in more than 14,200 clubs in 148 countries." Pretty impressive! I will bet your company would support you joining and attending Toastmasters.

Do you Know a Funny Story?

One of my more interesting Toastmaster experiences resulted when our club was holding a humorous speech contest. Three club members were scheduled to compete at our lunch hour club meeting, and the attendees would choose a winner who would go on to compete against winners from other Toastmaster clubs. If our winner went on to win against other clubs seven times, they would end up in Washington, DC, competing for the national Toastmasters humorous speech winners award.

When I got to the club meeting that day, our club president ran up to me and told me that one of the people who had signed up to make a humorous speech could not make it, and wanted to know if I knew any funny stories I could tell, just to round out the speaker's roster. I told him that I had been camping with my family the weekend before, and I had heard a campground ranger tell a hilarious story, that I could tell. So, he signed me up for the contest.

Well, the other two contestants gave their well-prepared five-minute humorous speeches, and then I recounted the ranger's funny story about a goldminer and a talking horse. The club voted, and I won. I was congratulated and informed that I would be representing our club at the regional toastmaster's humorous speech competition. I kept presenting that same silly story at subsequent competitions and won three more times.

Next thing I know, I am asked to compete with my story before 300 people on a Saturday afternoon in a large hotel ballroom in downtown Los Angeles. And… if I win, I am headed to San Jose, California, then on to Washington, DC. Now I am excited about this humorous speech contest and really getting into it.

Right before this competition is about to begin, all five of us competitors from clubs across Southern California are taken behind the stage and given a paper to sign. The essence of the paper was that you are about to give an original speech that you did not steal from anyone. I freaked out and ran to find my club president and remind him that I did not sign up for this competition, I had never read the rules, and he knew that I was recounting a story from a campground ranger.

My club president said, just sign it, I am sure you have embellished the story a little since you first heard it. I was a nervous wreck as I gave my speech, thinking *what if that campground ranger is in the audience, and stands up and yells out, "hey, that is my story!"* The end of this saga is that I ended up coming in second place, and the lady who won told a hilarious original story about dieting that definitely deserved to be first place.

People Who Can Make Good Presentations Get Promoted

My Toastmaster's payoff is that it definitely improved my management and speaking skills. I got many free lunches, and I networked with a group of interesting people who were outside of my industry. And after I retired, I wrote this book, and now I get paid to make presentations on how to turbocharge your career on your lunch hour. There is no question that I used my Toastmasters lunch experiences to turbocharge my career.

In *Inc.* magazine, Warren Buffett is quoted as saying *"One easy way to become worth 50 percent more than you are now, is to hone your communication skills – both written and verbal."*

We have established that improving your public speaking skills can have a significant positive impact on your career. Effective communication is a crucial skill in the professional world, and being a confident and articulate speaker can enhance your overall professional image. Here are some more ideas on how improving your public speaking skills, including participation in organizations like Toastmasters, can benefit your career:

1.   Enhanced Communication Skills:

     • Public speaking training helps you articulate your thoughts clearly and concisely. This skill is valuable in meetings, presentations, and everyday communication in the workplace.

2.   Increased Confidence:

     • As you develop your public speaking abilities, your confidence in expressing ideas and presenting information grows. Confidence is an attractive quality in leaders, and can positively influence how others perceive your competence.

3.   Leadership Opportunities:

     • Effective public speakers often are seen as leaders. As you become more skilled in public speaking, you may be entrusted with leadership roles and responsibilities within your organization.

4.   Career Advancement:

     • Individuals who can communicate persuasively and engage their audience are often considered for promotions and career advancement. Public speaking skills contribute to your professional profile, and can set you apart from your peers.

5. Successful Presentations:

    - Whether presenting to a small team or a large audience, the ability to deliver compelling and effective presentations is a valuable asset. It can lead to successful pitches, project proposals, and client interactions.

6. Networking Opportunities:

    - Public speaking engagements, conferences, and industry events provide opportunities to network with professionals in your field. Establishing yourself as a confident speaker can open doors to valuable connections and collaborations.

7. Improves Team Communication:

    - Strong public speaking skills translate into better communication within teams. The ability to convey ideas clearly fosters collaboration and teamwork, contributing to a more productive work environment.

8. Effective Communication with Clients:

    - For client-facing roles, being an effective communicator is crucial. Public speaking skills help you convey information, answer questions, and address concerns with clients, fostering trust and positive relationships.

9. Adaptability and Resilience:

- Public speaking requires adaptability and resilience. Learning to handle unexpected challenges during a speech or presentation helps build resilience, a valuable trait in the face of changing work environments.

In summary, improving your public speaking skills can contribute to your professional success by enhancing communication, building confidence, and opening doors to various career opportunities. Joining organizations like Toastmasters provides a structured and supportive platform for developing and refining these skills.

Learn a New Language

Maybe you want to use your newfound lunchtime to learn a new language. Use language learning apps like Duolingo or Babbel to pick up a new language. Consistency is key, and short daily sessions during lunch can be effective. *PC Magazine* claims Duolingo is the best free app for learning a new language or sharpening your skills. If you are serious about learning a new language, here are more details on the process. This will require a balance of focused study, practice, and exposure.

Start by taking a language proficiency test or use an app to assess your current level. This is a great way to understand your strengths and weaknesses in the language. Websites like Duolingo, Babbel, or Rosetta Stone often offer placement tests or assessments. Check if the language you are learning is supported on these platforms.

For those of you who want to take this to the next level, organizations such as the Common European Framework of Reference for Languages (CEFR) provide standardized language proficiency tests. Check if there's a specific test for the language you are learning. Contact language schools or universities to inquire about proficiency testing. Some institutions offer free language placement tests for learners.

It is important to hear native speakers, and practice. Spend 20-30 minutes engaging in interactive activities, like language exchange platforms or conversation practice. Reinforce what you've learned through real-world application. Remember to adapt this plan based on your personal preferences, the language you're learning, and the resources available to you. Consistency is key, so make learning enjoyable to maintain motivation during your lunchtime language sessions.

My personal experience with a foreign language is that I was born in the Dominican Republic. My American parents would live and work there for four years, then would come back to the USA for one year before returning again. Although I had visited the U.S., I did not move full time to the USA until I was 13 years old and in the eighth grade. I attended English-speaking schools in the Dominican Republic, but at recess and in our daily lives, we all spoke Spanish. As a kid, I was bilingual, but by the time I was an adult in mid-career, I was quickly losing my Spanish-speaking skills.

When I was 55 years old (this is 32 years after I had regularly used my 13-year-old Spanish vocabulary), the company I worked for (California Earthquake Authority) would regularly receive calls from Spanish speakers. The company needed a Spanish speaker to take an occasional Spanish call, and would pay an additional $100 a month to whomever could fill that role. Due to my upbringing, I obviously had a big head start on the goal of being fluent enough to take the Spanish calls, but I lacked confidence in my understanding and speaking skills. So, I went to the local library and checked out some conversational Spanish practice tapes, and started listening to them during my lunch hour. I also used this time to research the technical Spanish terms I would need to fulfill this role for an insurance company. My 13-year-old vocabulary did not include the Spanish words for earthquake (*terremoto*) or insurance (*Seguro*) or deductible (*deducible*) or insurance claim (*reclamación*).

When I felt I was ready, I applied for the role. They had an outside firm give me a test to see if I had sufficient Spanish comprehension and speaking skills. (That was nerve racking!) The test was given over the phone by a person at the testing company, and the test was proctored by the human resource person at my office. Proctored means I had to sit in her office so I couldn't cheat on the test. The tester started by giving me some easy Spanish sentences and asked me to translate them into English. For example: *¿Dónde está el baño?* Where is the bathroom? Next she gave me sentences in English, and I had to translate them into Spanish. For example: The judge (a female) will be late to work today. (Yikes, what is the Spanish word for a female judge?) *La jueza llegará tarde al trabajo hoy.*

Next, she would begin a sentence in Spanish, and I was to complete the sentence in Spanish. For example: *Si estuviera de vacaciones en México me gustaría…* (If I were on vacation in Mexico I would…) I answered: *"iria a la biblioteca."* ("I would go the library.") Under pressure, I couldn't think of anything meaningful to say at the time. She asked me "If I were president of the USA I would…" I answered, *"llevar a mi esposa a bailar,"* (take my wife dancing). Pretty weak, but I passed the test and was given the Spanish speaker role at work.

Thereafter I took all the Spanish calls at work. Interestingly, most Spanish speakers that I interacted with understand English, they just were not confident in speaking English. As a result, I would take the call and they would ask if I spoke Spanish. I would answer *"si,"* (yes in Spanish) and soon they were talking in Spanish, and I was talking in English, and since we both understood each other, we got along just fine.

Another part of my Spanish speaker role was to proofread all the marketing materials that they had translated into Spanish. This was way beyond my skill level, but being the resourceful guy that I am, I used Google Translate on the brochures that they had me review, and I came off looking like I really knew my stuff! It is not always about what you know, but that you know where to find what you need. (Let's keep this between us… they still think I am a Spanish Wiz!)

Several years later, the CEO of our company (three levels above me) was scheduled to speak as part of a panel at a conference in Mexico City, and at the last minute he couldn't go. Because he knew I was a Spanish Wiz, (my secret) he asked me to fill in for him, which I did. It was a great trip, and I got to hobnob with some very important people. The ex-president of the country of Columbia was on the same panel. I would not have had that opportunity if I had not put myself out there for the Spanish speaker role.

I can't point to any way specific that being the Spanish speaker at work turbocharged my career, other than there was a certain amount of prestige that went along with being that guy. My point to you is that if you have a foreign language skill or can learn a foreign language to a conversational level, you may be able to monetize it like I did.

Chapter 5 – Taking my Apple for a Walk at Lunch

"Be so good they can't ignore you. Competence is the ultimate passport to promotion." — Steve Martin

"Fresh air is like a natural elixir that invigorates both body and soul." — Unknown

During many lunch hours later in my career, I brought my lunch to work and would eat during the first 10 minutes of my lunch hour, and then go for a walk to get some fresh air and exercise. I generally packed an apple in my lunch, and would head to the building elevator with apple in hand. One day, someone asked me about the apple I was carrying into the elevator, and I told them I was taking my apple for a walk. It got to be a joke around the office. Whenever someone saw me with my apple on the way to the elevator, they would ask if I was taking my apple for a walk.

Using your lunch hour to get some exercise is a very good use of your lunchtime. But very few people do this. I often would see the same overweight people, sitting in the same chair in our lunchroom, munching on candy and potato chips, talking to the same people day, after day. What a wasted opportunity!

Explore Your Neighborhood

I viewed my personal lunchtime as an opportunity to go explore the neighborhoods around where I worked. I used to make it a game to see how far I could walk in one direction for 20 minutes, then turn around and get back to the office in the same time.

One day while I was out at lunch, and before I had eaten my apple, I was walking past a woman and a little boy of about five years old. (I think we now call them unhoused persons.) As I passed the lady, she asked for some money for food. I told her I couldn't give her any money, but if she would like, she could have this apple, and I held it out to her. The little boy jumped up and took the apple and starting munching on it like he was really hungry. That night I told my wife we needed to buy extra apples when we shopped, so I could take two apples with me for my lunch. One for me, and one to give away. The office where I was working at that time was in the downtown area of a large city, and from my walks around my office, I knew where the unhoused folks hung out. So, for the next month, I would eat my lunch and then take my two apples for a walk. It seemed like a good idea, but I had a really hard time giving away that second apple. I would ask people that looked like they could use some healthy nourishment if they would like an apple. Most said no, but could I spare some money? After a while, it was back to just me and my apple out for a walk.

Hanging Out With Duane

For part of my career, my office was in a downtown area with a fair amount of interesting street people out during my lunchtime. There was a nicely dressed man (about 40 years old) who sat all by himself on the same bench, on the same street, every day, and held out a paper cup requesting spare change from people walking by. When I asked him if he could use an apple, he said no, but would I please contribute to his paper cup fund. I said I couldn't contribute so he promptly cussed me out. There was plenty of room on his bench, so I sat down next to him. He didn't really want to talk, and so I just sat there and listened to him berate anyone who did not drop money in his cup, and then I said goodbye and left. In subsequent weeks whenever I saw him sitting on his bench, I would join him. He was not much for conversation, but over time I learned that his name was Duane, and he was not homeless because he had a room in the building next to his bench. He did not work because he said he was disabled. From my observation his disability was that he was socially awkward, and very angry at the world. He must have had a regular small income but he had nothing to do during the day, so for entertainment and extra income, he panhandled with his paper cup to all the business persons filing past his building every day.

I learned that he had no living mom and dad, or brothers or sisters. Or at least that is what he told me. I did not have any real purpose for hanging out with him, other than my fascination with how street people get to be street people.

One day I was out for a lunchtime walk with a business associate, and Duane walked past me and they were shocked when Duane said hello to me by name. I told them that he was a friend that I had made while taking my apple for a walk, and left it at that. At my retirement party some years later, that person mentioned my apple and that street person who called me by name. It reminded me that I had used part of my lunch hour to make Duane's life just a little bit more interesting. And if not his, at least it made my daily life more interesting.

Get Out of the Office

For a couple of years, I had a boss who would go out and buy lunch and a large iced tea, and then come back and sit at his desk in his office and work. (At least it looked like he was working. He may have been doing crossword puzzles or personal stuff.) I always felt sorry for him, because while I was out having fun, he was sitting at his desk. I need to remember, it is none of my business to wonder about what he does with his lunchtime, maybe that was his idea of fun.

My recommendation is get out and get some fresh air, a short walk, enjoy what nature there is around you, and you will feel more refreshed when you return for the afternoon.

Getting Exercise at Lunch

At one point in my career, there was a racquetball court close to where I worked and I, along with another guy from my office, often played racquetball at lunch. This required taking a shower before going back to work. These lunch hour excursions took longer than an hour, but by that time, I was in management and had the flexibility to take longer lunches as long as my department's work was getting done. The person I played with was our Corporate General Counsel. I had no reason to hang out with this lawyer, except for our common interest in racquetball. I never had occasion to interact with him at work, but I assume in meetings that I did not get invited to, if there had ever been an issue that affected me, he would have had my back. I am counting this as an unseen payback for the many fun racquetball lunchtimes I spent with him. I considered him part of my network, and it would not have occurred if I had not put myself out as a potential racquetball partner the first time he mentioned he played the game. Plus, it was fun and good exercise during lunch!

There was another time when I worked close to a golf course. I know golf is a poor excuse for exercise, but it sure is fun! In some professional settings, it might contribute positively to career development and potentially aid in getting promoted. I considered myself a corporate golfer. This means that I only played when there were golf outings sponsored by industry groups or corporate events. I did not play on weekends, because time with my kids and wife was more important to me than spending five hours every weekend at the local country club playing golf. But... I needed to keep my golf game up to a reasonable skill level so, about once a week, I would use my lunch hour to keep my golf skills up. The golf course close to where I worked had a chipping area where there were always a hundred golf balls laying around. I would take my pitching wedge and gather up a bucket of balls, and then chip them onto the chipping green. This didn't cost me anything, and was something I could do in one half hour. Another time I worked close to a shopping mall that had a sports store with an indoor driving range. It was mostly used to give golf lessons, but I could rent the range for one half hour and practice all my shots. So be creative, get out of the office, and find out what is available close to you!

You may not be a golfer, but if you are wondering *why play golf?* My research tells me here are some ways in which playing golf may be valuable to your career:

1. Networking Opportunities:

    - Golf is often considered a social sport and provides an excellent opportunity for networking. Many business deals and discussions happen on the golf course. Building relationships with colleagues and superiors outside the formal office setting can be beneficial for career growth.

2. Building Relationships With Superiors:

    - Golf outings may provide a more relaxed environment to interact with senior management or executives. Establishing a rapport with decision-makers outside the office can positively impact your professional image.

3. Team Building:

    - Golf is a sport that can be played in groups, making it an ideal activity for team building. Engaging in friendly competition or collaborative play with colleagues fosters a sense of camaraderie, which can contribute to a positive work environment.

4. Observing Professional Etiquette:

    - Golf is often associated with a set of social and professional etiquette. Playing the game can provide an opportunity to observe and demonstrate qualities, such as patience, sportsmanship, and respect – attributes that can be valued in a professional setting. Don't get mad and toss your clubs! That will reflect poorly on you.

5. Discussion Opportunities:

    - The time spent on the golf course can offer a more relaxed setting for discussions. Casual conversations during a round may lead to insights into the priorities and perspectives of colleagues and superiors.

6. Physical and Mental Well-Being:

    - Engaging in physical activity, such as walking on the golf course, can contribute to overall well-being. Physical health can positively impact mental health, leading to increased focus and productivity at work.

7. Work-Life Balance:

- Taking the time for leisure activities like golf can contribute to a healthy work-life balance. Demonstrating the ability to balance personal interests with professional responsibilities can be seen as a positive trait by employers.

8. Impressions of Commitment:

- In some corporate cultures, participating in activities like golf may be seen as a commitment to the organization's values and traditions. Demonstrating alignment with company culture can be influential in career advancement.

It's important to note that the impact of playing golf on career advancement can vary, based on the specific workplace culture, industry, and individual preferences of colleagues and superiors. While golf can offer valuable networking opportunities, it's essential to balance such activities with a focus on actual job performance and the development of relevant skills. Ultimately, the value of playing golf in a professional context depends on the dynamics of the workplace and the industry in which you work.

I know others who would go workout at a gym during lunch. At one point in my career, the CEO, who was three levels above me, used to go to the close-by gym during her lunch hour three days a week to work out. But, if it works for you, incorporating a workout routine during your lunchtime can bring several benefits to your overall well-being, and these positive effects can extend to your career in various ways. Here are some potential benefits:

1. Increased Energy and Productivity:

   - Regular physical activity has been shown to boost energy levels and enhance cognitive function. After a midday workout, you may find yourself more alert and focused, leading to increased productivity in the afternoon.

2. Stress Reduction:

   - Exercise is an effective stress reliever. Taking a break to work out during lunch can help you manage stress, reduce tension, and improve your overall mood. A less stressed and more relaxed mindset can positively impact your ability to handle work challenges.

3. Enhanced Mental Clarity:

   - Physical activity is linked to improved mental clarity and cognitive function. Clear thinking and mental sharpness are assets in making sound decisions and problem-solving at work.

4. Improved Health and Well-Being:

    - Regular exercise contributes to better physical health. When you prioritize your health, you are likely to experience fewer sick days and have more consistent energy levels, reducing the likelihood of burnout.

5. Building Healthy Habits:

    - Incorporating a lunchtime workout establishes a routine that promotes discipline and time management. Consistency in maintaining healthy habits can positively influence your work habits and approach to tasks.

6. Positive Impact on Team Dynamics:

    - If your workplace has a culture that encourages physical activity, working out during lunch can provide opportunities for team bonding. Participating in group workouts or encouraging colleagues to join you can foster positive relationships and camaraderie.

7. Demonstrating Work-Life Balance:

    - Prioritizing your health by exercising during lunch communicates a commitment to work-life balance. This commitment is increasingly valued by employers and can contribute to a positive perception of your overall work ethic.

8. Increased Job Satisfaction:

    *   Regular exercise has been linked to improved mood and increased feelings of well-being. Higher job satisfaction is often associated with greater engagement and longevity in a particular role or organization.

9. Networking Opportunities:

    *   If your workplace has fitness facilities or if there are nearby fitness classes, engaging in lunchtime workouts can provide networking opportunities with colleagues outside of formal work settings. Building relationships in a more casual environment can be valuable.

10. Enhanced Self-Confidence:

    *   Regular physical activity can contribute to improved physical fitness and overall well-being. Feeling good about your health and appearance can boost self-confidence, which can positively impact your interactions and communication in a professional setting.

Remember to consider your workplace culture and policies regarding lunch breaks and fitness activities. While many organizations encourage a healthy work environment, it's important to align your lunchtime workouts with the expectations and norms of your specific workplace.

Figure out what works for you and do it! If nothing else, find ways to use your lunch hour to get some exercise. A healthier body leads to a healthier mind, which leads to a healthier career.

82

Chapter 6 – Show Initiative

"Every accomplishment starts with the decision to try. Take the initiative and create your own opportunities." — Anonymous

"A journey of a thousand miles begins with a single step." — Lao Tzu

The Benefits of an Accountability Partner

Going through the ups and downs of any one career-enhancing effort can sometimes feel like a solo adventure. But imagine having a buddy by your side, cheering you on and helping you out. That's what we call an accountability partner, and it can make a big difference in your journey toward success. Let's explore why having an accountability partner can be a good thing for your career.

1. A Friend to Back You Up

    •   When you're working hard to move forward in your career, having a partner there to support you is like having a trusty sidekick. Your friend understand your goals and dreams, and is there to give you a boost when you need it. If you ever feel unsure or face tough challenges, your buddy can offer a fresh view and remind you that you've got what it takes.

2. Clear Goals and Better Focus

    •   An accountability partner helps you figure out exactly what you want to achieve in your career. By talking openly with your buddy, you can fine-tune your goals, and make sure they match your passions and values. This shared understanding helps you stay focused and work toward specific, doable targets.

3. More Motivation and Stick-to-itiveness

    •   Just knowing that someone is counting
        on you can be a big motivator.
        Accountability partners make you feel
        responsible, boosting your commitment
        to reaching your goals. Having a buddy
        to share the journey with creates
        a sense of teamwork and shared
        dedication, making it easier to keep
        going, even when things get tough.

4. Smarter Problem-Solving and Decision-
    Making

    •   Careers can be tricky, and you might
        face some tough choices along the
        way. That's where your buddy comes
        in handy as a thinking partner. Regular
        talks with your partner helps you think
        critically and consider different angles
        when you're dealing with challenges.
        Working together to solve problems can
        lead to smarter decisions and creative
        solutions.

5. Keeping Track of Your Progress

    •   One of the best things about having an
        accountability partner is that you can
        keep tabs on your progress. Regular
        check-ins create a routine for reviewing
        what you've achieved, what you're
        still working on, and where you can

improve. Celebrating your successes, no matter how small, becomes a shared victory, making you feel good about your journey.

6. Helpful Feedback for Growing

    *   Getting feedback is important for getting better at what you do, and your accountability partner is the perfect person to provide it. In a safe and supportive space, you can receive feedback on your work, find areas where you can improve, and discover new chances to grow. This mix of honest feedback and encouragement helps you learn and get better over time.

7. Beating Procrastination and Building Good Habits

    *   Procrastination (putting things off) can be a hurdle on your path to success. But with a buddy, you're less likely to delay tasks because you know someone is expecting you to make progress. This teamwork helps you build good habits and routines that are important for moving forward in your career.

8. More Friends and Chances to Work Together

- Having an accountability partner not only helps you personally but also opens doors to new opportunities. Through your buddy's connections, you get to know more people in your field and can even find chances to work together. This expanded network can give you useful advice, mentorship, and collaboration opportunities, making your journey to success even more exciting.

Having an accountability partner is like adding a special ingredient to your recipe for success. It makes your journey more exciting and helps you grow, not just in your career but also as a person. So, as you navigate the twists and turns of your career adventure, think about teaming up with a buddy – it's a boost that can make your climb to success even more fun and rewarding.

An accountability partner is a real-life concept. At one point in my career, I had a buddy in a different department, and we used to take a 15-minute walk during our afternoon breaks when our work schedules permitted. We were both career oriented and working on things to advance our careers. These walk and talk meetings generally involved sharing what we were doing to advance our careers, and checking in to see if we had followed through on the things we said we were working on. If your situation lends itself to having a regular meeting, formal or informal, with someone you trust, accountability partnership is a great thing to pursue.

Start a Lunchtime "Lunch and Learn"

This is not a new idea from me, but I had heard about companies who were regularly hosting a "Brown Bag Lunch and Learn." The concept is that anyone interested can bring their lunch into a conference room and listen to a speaker talk to everyone about a subject in which they have above average expertise. I received management approval to reserve and use the large conference room during one lunch hour a month. I recruited individuals in my office who had expertise in a specific area to be my presenters. I put out a schedule and invited everyone in my office to attend. This was an office of 120 people.

I had no problem keeping my speaker roster full, because most people have something they are good at, and they love sharing that knowledge in a non-threating environment. We usually had 5 to 20 attendees, depending on the topic. Some of the topics that were presented were: How to use PowerPoint, Microsoft Access, and most of the other general computer programs that were being used in our office. How to use GIS (graphic information systems) programs, and computer keyboard tips and tricks was another topic. I had managers from other departments come to tell us what they do. One presenter taught us how to read our corporate financial statements. No topic was off limits, if it was reasonably relevant. One lady did a session on how to train your dog. It was well attended.

The payoff for me was it showed initiative, I displayed organizational skills, and I learned a lot from the "Lunch and Learns" that I attended. I was able to network with executives from other departments, who heard about this program and were willing to come share their knowledge with our group.

If you decide to set up a Lunch and Learn program, here are several key steps to ensure its success.

Step 1: Define Objectives and Topics

Identify Goals: Determine the main objectives of the Lunch and Learn program. Goals could include knowledge sharing, team building, or professional development.

Select Topics: Choose relevant and engaging topics that align with the interests and needs of the participants. Consider subjects that can contribute to both personal and professional growth.

Step 2: Establish a Schedule and Format

Choose Frequency and Duration: Decide how often the Lunch and Learn sessions will occur (e.g., weekly, bi-weekly, monthly), and the duration of each session (typically 30 minutes to an hour).

Define Format: Determine the format of the sessions. This could include presentations, guest speakers, panel discussions, or interactive workshops.

Step 3: Identify Speakers and Facilitators

Source Internal and External Speakers: Identify individuals within your organization who can share expertise or experiences. Consider inviting external speakers or industry experts for diverse perspectives.

Establish a Speaker Calendar: Create a schedule of speakers, topics, and dates well in advance. This helps with planning and allows participants to know what to expect.

Step 4: Promote and Communicate

Create Marketing Materials: Develop promotional materials, such as posters, emails, or announcements to generate interest and inform employees about upcoming Lunch and Learn sessions.

Use Multiple Communication Channels: Utilize various communication channels, including email, company newsletters, and intranet platforms, to reach a wider audience.

Step 5: Organize Logistics

Choose a Suitable Location: Determine where the Lunch and Learn sessions will take place.

This could be a conference room, common area, or even virtually for remote teams.

Coordinate Lunch Options: Decide whether participants will bring their own lunches (brown bag), or if catering or delivery options will be provided. Ensure any dietary restrictions are considered.

Step 6: Facilitate Engagement

Encourage Participation: Foster a participatory environment. Encourage questions, discussions, and interaction between speakers and attendees.

Collect Feedback: Establish a mechanism for collecting feedback after each session. This feedback will help improve future Lunch and Learn events.

Step 7: Evaluate and Adjust

Analyze Participation and Impact: Regularly assess attendance rates, participant engagement, and the impact of each session on the overall goals of the program.

Make Adjustments: Use feedback and evaluation data to make adjustments to the program. This could include refining topics, changing formats, or addressing logistical issues.

Step 8: Celebrate Successes

Acknowledge Achievements: Recognize and celebrate successful Lunch and Learn sessions. Highlight positive feedback and the contributions of speakers and participants.

Share Success Stories: Share success stories and lessons learned with the broader organization. This can encourage continued participation and support.

By carefully planning each step and adapting based on feedback, you can create a Lunch and Learn program that enhances workplace learning, fosters team engagement, and contributes positively to the professional development of employees. And if you are the one running the show, you will be seen as one who takes the initiative, which is a very valuable and promotable trait.

Lose Weight and Get in Shape at Lunch

I had a co-worker who struggled to maintain a healthy weight. There was a WeightWatchers studio down the street from where we worked, and we would sometimes walk past it on our way to and from lunch. She was a self-starter, and she eventually signed up and would go there on a regular basis during her lunch hour. Lunchtime is a great time to address weight issues. On the Weightwatchers.com website they claim:

"Participate in live Virtual Workshops—they have a 97% satisfaction rating—or if there is a studio near you visit us for in-person workshops. Both options deliver expert coaching, scientific strategies, and inspiration on your journey. Join a live Kickstart orientation during your first week so you're on the right path, right from the beginning."

There are other lunchtime weight management programs and, if this is an issue for you, take the initiative and find a program that works for you. Your weight is a big part of your self-image, and this can play a big role in turbocharging your career. Here are some high-level tips that may be useful to you:

1. Hydrate:

    - Drink plenty of water throughout the day to stay hydrated and support weight loss.

2. Mindful Eating:

    - Eat slowly, savoring each bite. This helps with digestion and prevents overeating. (I am still working on this one. My wife says I eat like a fireman going to a fire.)

3. Healthy Snacks:

    - Keep nutritious snacks (nuts, fruits, yogurt) at your desk to avoid reaching for unhealthy options.

4. Meal Prep:

    - Plan and prepare your meals in advance to ensure they align with your weight loss goals.

Lifestyle Changes

1. Desk Exercises:

    - Incorporate simple desk exercises, like leg lifts or seated stretches, to stay active during work hours.

2. Take Short Walks:

    - Use part of your lunch break for a short walk, either indoors or outdoors.

3. Manage Stress:

    - Practice stress management techniques, such as deep breathing, meditation, or quick mindfulness exercises.

4. Sleep Well:

    - Ensure you get enough sleep each night to support overall health and weight loss.

Remember, consistency is key, and it's crucial to listen to your body. Consult with a healthcare professional or fitness expert before starting any new exercise or weight loss program, especially if you have underlying health conditions.

Boss the Boss

Here is an idea that is not related to the "Turbocharge Your Career on your lunch hour" strategy, but was so successful in my career that I share it at no extra cost. I was transferred to an insurance policy processing company in Denver, Colorado, where I was the manager of a group of 60 people that included managers and supervisors. I didn't know them, and they didn't know me. As a way for me to get up to speed about what they did, and for the employees to get to know me, I started a "Boss the Boss" program.

Every Wednesday afternoon I would spend two hours doing someone's job. That employee got to show me what they did, and boss me around for two hours. I asked the supervisors to make a schedule with every person in our group for a Wednesday afternoon two-hour boss-the-boss session. This was in 1992, so some of the functions I performed don't even exist today, but you will get the idea. It took a little over a year to complete the program.

I started in the filing department and an entry-level employee who had been there less than a year got to have me do her job for two hours. So, for those two hours, I filed paper into manila folders on shelves.

I worked in a word processing department where other departments dictated their correspondence into a computer, and word processors would type up the letters. I happen to be a good typist, so for two hours I sat there with headphones on and transcribed letters.

As you can imagine, some employees were afraid of having their manager come sit at their desk and do their job. The supervisors were afraid I would discover something they should have fixed long ago. But for each employee that I sat with, I humbled myself and told them that I was their personal assistant for the next two hours, and I wanted them to teach me what they did and have me actually perform the functions they did. After several weeks, the word got out that it was not a scary thing, and that I was not looking to make trouble. We had fun with this, and some even looked for the most menial part of their jobs for me to perform. (Perhaps they thought I couldn't handle anything too complicated.)

The beauty of the program was my employees got to know me as a real down-to-earth person. I got to learn and see what they were doing. There were times when I asked why we did that, and often it was *because we have always done it that way*, or *that is how I was trained*. Occasionally, after my two-hour session, I would talk to their supervisor in private and sometimes we eliminated some unnecessary functions. We also bought some new equipment for people who were working with broken equipment, so their jobs were improved.

Some years later I was transferred from Denver to the Sacramento, California, office. When I got to

Sacramento, I did not know any of the supervisors or employees, so as a way to get to know everyone and for them to get to know me, I started the "Boss-the-Boss" program again. I really enjoyed doing this, and I think it was very useful to my management progression in the company.

What if You Work From Home?

We had a phenomenon due to the COVID-19 pandemic that has caused many people (bosses and employees) to learn that they can, in fact, effectively work from home. This brings up the question about how you can turbocharge your career on your lunch-hour if you work from home.

The work-from-home people that I have spoken with tell me that you must be more purposeful with your free time, i.e. lunch hour, when you work from home. If you are not careful, you will end up doing laundry during lunch, dealing with homeschooled kids, going shopping, etc.

These are all good things. However, the goal is to get ourselves better prepared to take on new responsibilities without using before and after work hours. You at-home workers must look hard for opportunities to stay connected so you can advance in your career. Here is some advice and a few tips:

1. Virtual Networking:

    -   Actively participate in virtual meetings, webinars, and industry events to stay connected with colleagues and industry professionals.

- Join online forums, LinkedIn groups, and other professional networks to engage in discussions and expand your network.

2. Regular Check-Ins:

- Schedule regular virtual check-ins with your team and supervisor to maintain communication and alignment on tasks and projects.

- Use video calls whenever possible to enhance personal connections.

3. Online Learning Platforms:

- Take advantage of online learning platforms to acquire new skills and knowledge relevant to your role or industry.

- Discuss your learning goals with your manager to align them with the company's objectives.

4. Professional Development:

- Seek out virtual workshops, conferences, and training sessions to enhance your professional development.

- Consider certifications or courses that can contribute to your career growth.

5. Remote Team Building:

    - Organize virtual team-building activities to foster a sense of camaraderie and collaboration among team members.

    - Use collaboration tools effectively to maintain a sense of unity, despite physical distance.

6. Visibility and Recognition:

    - Actively communicate your achievements and contributions to your team and superiors.

    - Seek feedback regularly and showcase your dedication to your work.

7. Career Conversations:

    - Schedule virtual one-on-one meetings with your manager to discuss your career goals and seek guidance on your professional development.

    - Inquire about opportunities for advancement within the company.

8. Balance and Well-being:

    - Establish clear boundaries between work and personal life to prevent burnout.

    - Take breaks and practice self-care to maintain mental and physical well-being.

Remember that connection and communication is key in a remote work setting, and being proactive in seeking out opportunities for learning, networking, and career growth is essential.

If you work from home, it may be more difficult, since you are probably located in a neighborhood, rather than a commercial or industrial area. As a result, you will not have easy access to some of the opportunities I had with Toastmasters, industry lunch meetings, etc. Be creative and find what works for you, so you too can make the most of your lunch hours.

Only time will tell, and I look forward to hearing from you on this topic.

Chapter 7 - Lunchtime Enrichment Activities

"Seriousness may build the foundation, but it's the lightness of laughter and the playfulness of joy that add the colors to life's canvas. Don't be afraid to splash a little fun into your masterpiece."
— Anonymous

"The things that enrich our lives are not possessions but experiences, relationships, and the memories we create along the way." — Unknown

Not everything you do during your lunch hour needs to be focused on turbocharging your career. It is OK and, in fact, advisable to do some fun things at lunch whenever possible. An interesting person is always more desirable when bosses are looking to promote someone.

I will share a few of the fun things I was able to do during my lunch hours. Over my 45-year career, as I moved with different companies in different locations, different opportunities presented themselves. And many of these only lasted for several years until my circumstances changed. But whenever I landed in a new place, I would take my apple for a walk to discover what interesting lunchtime activities existed in my new lunch hour space.

Museums

When I worked in Los Angeles, for a time I worked at 5757 Wilshire Blvd., which is very close to the Los Angeles County Museum of Art. Here is what Wikipedia says about LACMA:

> *"The Los Angeles County Museum of Art is an art museum located on Wilshire Boulevard in the Miracle Mile vicinity of Los Angeles. LACMA is on Museum Row, adjacent to the La Brea Tar Pits. LACMA is the largest art museum in the western United States. It attracts nearly a million visitors annually."*

Pretty impressive, don't you think? I had to walk through the La Brea Tar Pits to get to the museum. Here is what Wikipedia says about the La Brea Tar Pits:

"La Brea Tar Pits are a group of tar pits around which Hancock Park was formed in urban Los Angeles. Natural asphalt has seeped up from the ground in this area for tens of thousands of years. The tar is often covered with dust, leaves, or water. Over many centuries, the tar preserved the bones of trapped animals." These bones are displayed in the Tar Pit Museum.

I learned that one day a month the museums were free. I liked going to the museums on their free days and, if possible, I would join a docent tour. I found out that some of my co-workers had never been to either museum. I guess they did not understand the concept of making yourself a more interesting person, which was part of turbocharging your career on your lunch hour. It turned out that I only worked at this location for two years. How sad it would have been if I had not availed myself of this amazing history and culture during my two years at that location.

For the LACMA, I found out what time their docent-guided tours started, then adjusted my lunch hour accordingly. I always told the docent ahead of time not to be offended when I left early, because I was on my lunch hour and would have to bail out of the tour after 45 minutes.

Shopping

At one point I worked about a five-minute walk to Costco, a membership-only warehouse club. Our company gave every employee access to corporate membership, so we could go in for free. And, every Friday Costco had people giving out free samples of food items. That became a Friday lunch for some of my co-workers and me. I am not sure what this did for my career, but I love free lunches, and I spent a fair amount of time picking the brains of the tech folks in the TV, camera, and personal computer department.

Farmers Market

At another place I worked, there was a farmer's market in a nearby park every Wednesday. I often shopped for fresh produce including walking apples, which always made my wife happy when I brought them home in the evening. There usually were street musicians playing at the farmer's market, so it was fun to take my lunch, and sit on the grass and listen to the music during my lunch hour.

Historic Buildings

Once in Sacramento, during my lunch walk, I ran into a group of about 20 people who appeared to be on a tour. I approached one of the guys on the tour, and he told me it was the Building Manager Association, and they were touring the top floors of the 10 most impressive buildings in Sacramento. I asked, "Any chance I could tag along?" and to my surprise, he said yes, I could be his guest.

I knew my meeting schedule back at the office was clear, so I called my boss and asked him if I could have a longer lunch. This was the eat-at-his-desk guy, and he knew about some of the crazy stuff I did on my lunch hours, so he approved my being out of the office for a while. I spent the next several hours with the group, which never even asked who I was or why I was there. This was right after Arnold Schwarzenegger was no longer governor of California, and I got to see his private suite and cigar smoking balcony high up in the Hyatt Hotel. I also got to hear the interesting story of an eccentric bank manager who, before they built his bank building, put himself in a construction bucket hanging from a crane so he could determine exactly how high his top floor office needed to be so he could have the best view of the Sacramento Waterfront. It was interesting to me and has made for some good stories over the years.

My office in Sacramento, California, was about seven blocks from the Old Town Sacramento Waterfront on the Sacramento River. Amazingly, there were people in my office who never went there. Following is some of the amazing history they were missing out on:

Gold Rush Legacy — Old Town Sacramento originated during the Gold Rush of the mid-1850s.

It was a major commercial and transportation hub during this period, serving as a gateway to the goldfields.

Historic Architecture — The waterfront area features well-preserved historic buildings and wooden sidewalks, giving visitors a glimpse into the architecture of the Gold Rush era.

Attractions and Points of Interest — The Delta King is a historic riverboat docked along the Sacramento River. The Delta King is a hotel, restaurant, and entertainment venue.

The waterfront is part of the larger Old Sacramento State Historic Park. The park encompasses numerous museums, shops, and attractions dedicated to preserving the history of the region.

This area is home to the Sacramento History Museum, which provides exhibits and interactive displays that delve into the city's past, including the Gold Rush and railroad history. This one is free.

The California State Railroad Museum is one of the most popular attractions in Old Town, showcasing the history of the railroad in California. Visitors can explore historic locomotives and railroad cars. Climbing into them is fun for all ages.

There is a waterfront promenade with views of the Sacramento River. The area is beautifully landscaped and offers benches for relaxation. There were many lunch hours in which I ate my lunch there instead of at work.

The Old Sacramento Waterfront hosts various events throughout the year, including festivals, live music, and family-friendly activities. I especially loved it in the fall during Gold Rush Days festival when they would bring in 70 tons of dirt to cover all the streets. Then locals would dress in period costumes, so you could imagine what it was like to live back then, including mock gun fights.

There is waterfront dining at various restaurants offering a range of cuisines. Many establishments have outdoor seating with views of the river. After your meal, you can visit an array of unique shops and boutiques where you'll find everything from souvenirs to handmade crafts. I especially loved killing time in the kite store.

California State Capitol

My Sacramento office was about three blocks from the California State Capitol building. During one lunch hour, I took a tour of the Capitol building. The 1870s history and architecture were beautiful and fascinating. Since the Capitol building is a public space, I would often wander around the building during my lunch hour. Arnold Schwarzenegger was governor at the time, so I walked to his office to see what it looked like. There was a reception area where his secretary sat. When I saw his business cards on her desk, I asked for and was given a handful. I was a big hit with the friends I gave his business card to! I think my brother still carries an Arnold card in his wallet, which he proudly shows to friends claiming that his brother (me) knew Arnold. Not true, but fun nonetheless.

Botanical Tour

Another time I took a guided tour of all the trees planted in the adjoining Capitol Park. There are many from all over the world. We saw a redwood tree with a sign on it that read "Moon Tree." It turns out that in January 1971 Apollo 14 was the third trip by the U.S. to the lunar surface. Alan Shepard and Edgar Mitchell walked on the Moon while Stuart Roosa, a former U.S. Forest Service smoke jumper, orbited above in the command module. Packed in small containers in Roosa's personal kit were hundreds of redwood tree seeds, part of a joint NASA/USFS project.

Upon return to Earth, the seeds were sent to the Southern Forest Service station in Gulfport, Mississippi, and to the Western station in Placerville, California, to attempt germination. Surprisingly, nearly all the seeds germinated successfully, and the Forest Service now had some 420 tree seedlings to dispose of. Known as the "Moon Trees," the resulting seedlings were given away and planted throughout the United States as part of the nation's bicentennial in 1976. A redwood tree in Sacramento had been one of those seedlings.

Free Concerts

For the month of December every year, there are free lunchtime concerts in the rotunda of the California State Capitol. I often walked there to listen to music. One of the funniest concerts I saw was given by a group from a retirement home for military veterans. The old-timers had no musical talent, but they sure had fun. They were singing and playing ukuleles, spoons, kazoos, drums, blocks of wood, and having a blast, which made it fun for everyone. My lunch buddies and I had some laughs watching those old-timers play for us.

After I retired, I moved to an "active adult" community in the Sacramento area called Heritage Park. My new community has a band made up of retired folks who played an instrument back in their youth. I play the tenor banjo, so I joined the Heritage Park Band. And, wouldn't you know it, our band now plays in the California State Capitol rotunda during Christmas lunchtimes. I am assuming some of the spectators get some good laughs watching us old-timers play for them. Here is a YouTube link of our band performing at the Capitol building during Christmas 2023. https://www.youtube.com/watch?v=Ntf04DbAGao

There was a beautiful stone Presbyterian church about five blocks from my office in downtown Sacramento. While out walking at lunch, I saw the message board in front of the church advertising a free noontime concert every Thursday. It encouraged people to bring a lunch and eat it in the church during the concert. I assumed that once I entered, I would be cornered and asked for money, or asked to join their church. But to my surprise, when I went in they greeted me, gave me a bag of popcorn, and invited me to sit anywhere. I opted for the balcony so I could quietly leave in order to get back to my office before my hour's lunch was up. I soon learned that the concerts were performed by visiting artists from all over the world. Some of the world music was very unusual, but all of it was performed by super talented musicians. This was a great way to spend a lunch hour broadening my musical horizons.

Lunchtime Bible Study

One day at lunchtime in downtown Sacramento, I was wandering through the Capitol building hallways killing time, and I saw a sign for a non-denominational Bible Study being held once a week from noon to 1 p.m. by the Capitol Chaplin. I popped my head in the conference room and was warmly greeted by about 15 people, so I stayed for the rest of my lunch hour. I really enjoyed the Capitol Chaplin's teaching, and getting to know the political movers and shakers who also attended. What really intrigued me was every time there was a contentious issue before the legislature (abortion, authority of the government, LGBQT, death penalty, etc.) he would present what the Bible said about that issue.

His teaching sessions were often a bi-partisan tightrope walk on sensitive subjects, but as a believer, I enjoyed his presentations and the discussions that resulted. This was just one of those serendipitous opportunities that you must keep your eyes open for and, when you find them, take advantage if it interests you.

Chapter 8 –
Traits of Successful People

"He that is good for making excuses is seldom good for anything else." — Ben Franklin

"Seek opportunities, not guarantees. Taking risks is the key to unlocking your career potential."
— Anonymous

Get Organized on Your Lunch Hour

Successful people are organized. If your desk or work area is a mess, use your lunchtime to get your data and paper under control. Organizing your desk at work is a great way to boost productivity, and create a more efficient and pleasant working environment. Here's a step-by-step plan to help you get your desk organized:

Step 1 — Set Clear Goals:
Define what you want to achieve with an organized desk. Whether it's to improve productivity, reduce stress, make time for career-enhancing turbocharge activities, or create a more professional appearance. Having clear goals will guide your organizing process.

Step 2 — Declutter:
Start by removing everything from your desk. Sort through the items and decide what you need and what you can do without. Discard unnecessary items, and only keep essentials.

Step 3 — Categorize Items:
Group similar items together. Create categories based on the nature of the items, such as office supplies, personal items, project materials, etc. This will make it easier to find things later on.

Step 4 — Prioritize Essentials:
Identify the essential items you need on a daily basis, and ensure they have a designated and

easily accessible space on your desk. Items that are less frequently used can be stored in drawers or on shelves.

Step 5 — Invest in Organizational Tools:
Consider using organizational tools, such as trays, containers, drawer organizers, and file holders. These tools can help you keep things in order and make it easier to maintain a tidy workspace.

Step 6 — Create a Filing System:
Organize your documents using a filing system that makes sense to you. Label folders clearly, and consider using color-coding for different projects or categories. A well-organized filing system will save you time and reduce stress.

Step 7 — Utilize Digital Organization:
If possible, digitize documents and notes to reduce paper clutter. Organize your computer files into folders, and regularly clean up your digital workspace.

Step 8 — Establish a Daily Routine:
Develop a routine for maintaining your organized desk. Spend a few minutes at the end of each day decluttering and organizing. This will prevent the accumulation of unnecessary items and maintain a clean workspace.

Step 9 — Personalize Thoughtfully:
Add personal touches to your desk, but do so thoughtfully. Consider using items that inspire or motivate you, but avoid overcrowding your workspace with too many personal items.

Step 10 — Regular Maintenance:
Set aside time on a regular basis to reassess and maintain your organized desk. Adjust your system as needed, and be proactive in preventing clutter from building up.

By following these steps, you can create an organized and efficient workspace that promotes productivity and a sense of well-being.

The Vicious Cycle of Procrastination

In your journey for professional growth, procrastination emerges as a formidable adversary, silently sabotaging aspirations and impeding the journey toward career advancement. This seemingly harmless delay tactic can have profound and detrimental effects on one's professional trajectory.

Procrastination, often disguised as a fleeting delay or a momentary diversion, can quickly evolve into a pervasive pattern that erodes productivity, and stunts personal and professional development. The first detrimental effect of procrastination lies in its ability to create a self-reinforcing loop. When tasks are delayed, they accumulate, creating an overwhelming backlog that intensifies stress and anxiety. As the pressure mounts, individuals may resort to further procrastination as a coping mechanism, perpetuating a cycle that hinders progress.

Procrastination is a silent thief of potential, robbing individuals of the precious time needed to realize their ambitions. By putting off crucial tasks, opportunities for growth and advancement slip through the fingers. Aspiring professionals may find themselves stuck in a perpetual cycle of unfulfilled goals, leading to frustration, self-doubt, and a sense of stagnation in their careers.

In the collaborative landscape of the modern workplace, procrastination can strain professional relationships and impede teamwork. When one's tasks are consistently delayed, it places an undue burden on colleagues and team members who may need to pick up the slack. This strain can erode trust and camaraderie, potentially limiting future collaborative opportunities and diminishing the overall effectiveness of the team.

The toll of procrastination extends beyond the confines of the workplace, seeping into the mental and emotional well-being of individuals. Constantly deferring tasks can lead to heightened stress, anxiety, and a persistent feeling of being overwhelmed. The weight of unfinished responsibilities can become a heavy burden, affecting not only professional performance but also one's overall quality of life.

While the consequences of procrastination are significant, the good news is that it is a habit that can be broken. Let's explore some effective techniques to conquer procrastination, and pave the way for a more successful career journey.

1. Set Clear and Achievable Goals

   - The foundation for overcoming procrastination begins with setting clear and achievable goals. Break down larger tasks into smaller, more manageable steps. Establishing specific, measurable, and time-bound objectives provides a roadmap for action, making it easier to tackle tasks without feeling overwhelmed.

2. Prioritize Tasks and Create a Schedule

   - Prioritization is a powerful antidote to procrastination. Evaluate tasks based on their importance and urgency, and create a schedule that allocates dedicated time for each. Having a structured plan fosters a sense of control, helping you navigate through your responsibilities systematically.

3. Break Tasks into Manageable Chunks

   - Large projects or tasks can be intimidating, leading to procrastination. Break them down into smaller, more manageable chunks. Focusing on completing one segment at a time makes the overall goal seem less daunting, encouraging a steady and consistent approach. I always had a "to do" list on my desk with items labeled A, B, C, depending on priority. It feels good to cross off each small item as it is accomplished.

4. Utilize Time Management Techniques

    - Effective time management is a key weapon in the battle against procrastination. Techniques such as the **Pomodoro Technique**, in which work is divided into intervals with short breaks in between, can enhance focus and productivity. Experiment with different time management methods to discover what works best for your individual work style.

Your job may not lend itself to this, but if you are curious, here is a recap of the Pomodoro Technique. It is a time-management method developed by Francesco Cirillo in the late 1980s. The technique is named after the Italian word for "tomato," because Cirillo initially used a tomato-shaped kitchen timer to track his work intervals. The method is designed to improve efficiency and focus by breaking work into intervals, traditionally 25 minutes in length, separated by short breaks. Here's how the Pomodoro Technique typically works:

- Select a task or project that you want to work on.

- Set a timer for 25 minutes (this is one Pomodoro). During this time, focus exclusively on the chosen task and work with intensity.

- Work on the task until the timer rings, signaling the end of the 25-minute interval.

- Take a short break, around five minutes. Use this time to stretch, take a quick walk, or do something unrelated to work.

- Repeat the process. After completing four Pomodoros, take a longer break of around 15–30 minutes.

The key principles of the Pomodoro Technique include:

- Breaking the work into intervals helps manage time more effectively and reduces the likelihood of burnout.

- The technique encourages deep focus during the 25-minute intervals, promoting a state of flow where productivity and creativity thrive.

- Short breaks between intervals help prevent mental fatigue and maintain overall productivity throughout the day.

While the traditional Pomodoro interval is 25 minutes, some individuals may find that adjusting the length of the Pomodoro to suit their attention span works better for them. The Pomodoro Technique is widely used and appreciated for its simplicity and effectiveness. It's a versatile tool that can be applied to various tasks, from studying and writing, to coding and project management. Many people find that breaking work into manageable intervals helps them stay focused, avoid distractions, and maintain a steady pace of productivity.

1. Cultivate a Positive Mindset

   - Procrastination often thrives in a negative mindset. Cultivate a positive outlook by focusing on the benefits of completing tasks, and envisioning the positive outcomes of your efforts. Celebrate small victories along the way, reinforcing a positive association with taking action.

2. Minimize Distractions and Create a Productive Environment

   - Identify and minimize potential distractions in your workspace. Turn off notifications, create a clutter-free environment, and establish a designated area for work. A focused and organized workspace can significantly reduce the temptation to procrastinate.

3. Embrace the 2-Minute Rule

    •   If a task takes two minutes or less to complete, tackle it immediately. The 2-Minute Rule is a simple but effective strategy to prevent small tasks from accumulating and becoming sources of procrastination.

4. Leverage Accountability Partnerships

    •   Enlisting the support of an accountability partner can be a game-changer in overcoming procrastination. Sharing your goals and progress with someone else creates a sense of responsibility and encouragement. Regular check-ins with your partner provide external motivation and a gentle nudge to stay on track.

5. Address Underlying Issues

    •   Procrastination can sometimes be a symptom of underlying issues, such as fear of failure, perfectionism, or lack of confidence. Addressing these root causes through self-reflection, counseling, or professional development can contribute to a more proactive and resilient mindset.

Breaking free from the chains of procrastination requires a commitment to cultivating habits that promote consistent action. By setting clear goals, prioritizing tasks, and adopting practical strategies, individuals can overcome the detrimental effects of procrastination, and unleash their full potential in the pursuit of a successful and fulfilling career. Remember, the power to transform your professional journey lies in your hands – act today and witness the positive impact on your career trajectory.

Read During Lunch

Inc. magazine notes that Warren Buffett taught: *"…Go to bed a little smarter each day."*

The fact that Buffett has achieved so much means his advice is highly sought after. He thinks anyone can do the same if they follow one simple rule: the Buffett Formula. According to Buffett, the key to your success is to go to bed a little smarter each day. Buffett pointed out the strong similarity with investing when he said, "That's how knowledge builds up. Like compound interest."

One of the ways he famously builds his knowledge is to read. A lot. While Buffett has been known to spend 80 percent of his daily routine reading, whether or not you have time for such an ambitious goal is largely irrelevant. The point of the Buffett Formula is to make whatever progress you can and improve your life on a daily basis.

Here is a tip: If you walk by your boss's desk and see a book about management or self-improvement, read that same book. Lunch time is a great time to read. Feed your mind while you are feeding your body. There are tons of self-help books that you can check out from the library or download to your reading device. The why behind reading what your boss is reading is that it gives you a common point of interest that may allow for a discussion with your boss that you would not have otherwise had the opportunity to have.

I once had a boss who was always reading the latest management guru book. He advocated for his subordinates to read those same books and even went so far as to give us copies to read. At that point in my career, I wasn't all that excited about reading those books, but I read them, and we discussed them, and I am sure that over time it helped me develop my management skills. Beyond that, this boss appreciated my dedication to self-improvement, and I am sure that reading those books had a positive effect somewhere throughout the arc of my career.

I use Libby to read books on my smartphone and on my tablet. (I have an Apple iPad.) Libby is a popular free library app that allows users to borrow and read books or listen to audiobooks from their local public library. Libby is user-friendly and available for both Android and iOS devices. Libby is a whole lot more convenient than carrying around a printed book. I find that I read more now that I can get any book free on my tablet. I also can download magazines from Libby, and can read *National Geographic, Inc.* magazine, and *Popular Mechanics* free every month on my Libby app. A subscription to *National Geographic* is currently $29 a year, *Inc.* magazine is $19.99, and *Popular Mechanics* is $19 a year. Libby sends me a notice every time a new magazine is released. It doesn't cost me anything. It's a great lunchtime filler.

Here's an overview of how to use Libby:

1. Download the Free App:

   - Visit the App Store (iOS) or Google Play Store (Android) on your device.

   - Search for "Libby" and download the app.

2. Open the App:

   - Launch the Libby app on your device.

3. Sign In:

   - You will need to sign in using your library card. If you don't have a library card, you can visit your local library to obtain one. You also can apply online for a library card through your local library.

Browsing and Borrowing Books:

1. Search for Titles or Authors:

- Use the search bar to find specific books or browse through various genres and collections.

2. Borrowing Books:

- Once you find a book you want, click on "Borrow" or "Place Hold" if the book is currently checked out. If placing a hold, you'll receive a notification when the book becomes available.

Reading and Listening:

1. Read or Listen In-App:

- After borrowing, you can read ebooks directly in the app or listen to audiobooks.

2. Customization:

- Adjust font size, background color, and other settings for a personalized reading experience. If the room is dark, choose the dark background with white letters. If you are reading in a very bright area, choose the white background with black letters. I also love that I can increase the size of the font, so my eyes don't have to work as hard as they do to read some of the small fonts found in books.

3. Return Items:

- You can renew books that you have not finished, and books are automatically returned when the loan period expires, so there are no late fees.

Libby offers a seamless and convenient way to access digital books from your local library. Keep in mind that the features and functionality may vary slightly, depending on your library's specific setup and the availability of digital titles in their collection.

Libby also allows you to connect to more than one library. The reason you might want to do this is if your local library doesn't have the book you want, another library may have it. You sign up for a library card from every library you want to access. For example, I have a library card from the Sacramento Public Library, but I could get library cards from Los Angeles and San Francisco if I wanted. In your Libby app, go to menu and tap "add library," then search that library for your book.

If you don't like to read, remember you can listen to audio books on Libby. I have convinced myself that I should read rather than listen to books, because I think it keeps my brain young. But, many of my friends prefer to listen to books, and you should do whatever suits you best. Obviously, if you are a long-haul trucker, you should listen rather than read while driving!

Also, for you audio listeners, you can download free podcasts to your smartphone and listen while you enjoy your lunch. Start with the podcast called *Stuff You Should Know.* It's free and will make you a more interesting conversationalist. They claim it is "The best darn podcast in the land! If you've ever wanted to know about champagne, satanism, the Stonewall Uprising, chaos theory, LSD, El Nino, true crime, and Rosa Parks, then look no further. Josh and Chuck have you covered." I thoroughly enjoy it.

At one point in my career, I worked several blocks from a brick-and-mortar library. I often would walk to the library and, because I did not have a lot of time, I usually went to the periodicals, and sat and looked at a magazine. When I was re-doing my back yard, I read landscaping magazines during my visit.

Successful People Teach

I am sure you know that you will learn more from teaching than any other learning activity. I once worked for a company that had a policy that if someone attended an industry conference, they had to come back and teach something they had learned. That was a successful principle. I found a conference I really wanted to attend, so I got permission to go, and when I came back, I taught a class to my peers. I had taken better notes, and learned the material better since I knew I had to teach it, and my peers respected me for my teaching. This also made me realize that I enjoyed teaching!

It is a proven fact that teaching can contribute to the development of various skills and experiences that can positively impact your career. Here are some ways in which teaching can be beneficial for your professional growth:

1. Deepens Understanding: Teaching requires a thorough understanding of the subject matter. Explaining concepts to others forces you to clarify your own understanding, leading to a deeper and more comprehensive knowledge of the material.

2. Communication Skills: Teaching hones your communication skills. You learn how to convey complex ideas in a clear and concise manner, adapting your communication style to different audiences.

3. Adaptability: As a teacher, you often encounter diverse learning styles and levels of understanding. This experience helps you become more adaptable and skilled at tailoring your approach to meet the needs of different individuals or groups.

4. Leadership Skills: Taking on the role of an instructor involves leadership. You guide others in their learning journey, manage classrooms, and may even lead educational initiatives. These experiences contribute to the development of leadership skills.

5. Problem-Solving Abilities: Teaching requires the ability to assess and address challenges in the learning process. This enhances your

problem-solving skills as you find creative ways to explain concepts and help students overcome difficulties.

6. Networking Opportunities: Teaching often involves interacting with students, colleagues, and other professionals in the education field. This provides networking opportunities that can be valuable for your career, helping you connect with like-minded individuals, mentors, or potential collaborators.

7. Builds Credibility and Authority: Being a teacher in a particular subject area can enhance your credibility and authority in that field. This can lead to opportunities for public speaking, writing, or consulting within your area of expertise.

8. Professional Development: Engaging in teaching often requires ongoing professional development to stay current with educational trends and methodologies. This commitment to learning can be attractive to employers and enhance your marketability.

9. Enhances Time Management Skills: Juggling lesson planning, grading, and teaching demands effective time management. This skill is transferable to many professions, in which the ability to prioritize tasks and manage time efficiently is crucial.

10. Personal Satisfaction and Fulfillment: Teaching can be personally rewarding. The satisfaction of helping others learn and succeed can contribute to a sense of fulfillment, which can positively impact your overall job satisfaction and well-being.

While teaching can bring numerous benefits to your career, it's important to note that the extent of these advantages may vary, depending on the context, your commitment to teaching, and how well it aligns with your overall career goals.

Work on Your Side Hustle

Invest time in nurturing your side hustle. If you're engaged in a personal project or side business, consider allocating a portion of your lunch break to its development. This could involve tasks like building a website, working on a creative project, or writing a book. While it might initially feel unconventional, dedicating your extra time to longstanding ideas, such as a book or business venture, can be immensely rewarding.

Exercise caution to ensure you're not diverting time or resources from your primary job. Avoid using company equipment like the photocopier for personal business, and be mindful not to compromise the hours your employer is compensating you for. It's crucial not to jeopardize your current position prematurely; you want to ensure a smooth transition when you're ready to pursue your independent venture.

Chapter 9 –
Can We Change Any of These

"Don't be busy; be productive. Focus on what matters most for career progression."
— Anonymous

"Change is the law of life. And those who look only to the past or present are certain to miss the future." — John F. Kennedy

Before we can decide what kinds of turbocharge activities we will work on during our lunch hours, we need to take a few minutes to break our "work-self" down into its many parts. Then we will look at each part to see if it can be impacted by a change in our lunch-hour activity.

The following chapter may feel like drinking from a fire hose, so find what you need most and ignore the rest.

Healthy Body

Every one of us needs a high-energy healthy body in order to do our best work. The connection between physical health and work efficiency is well-established, as the two are closely intertwined. Maintaining good physical health can have a significant impact on various aspects of work performance. Here are several ways in which physical health and work efficiency are connected:

In *Inc.* magazine, Warren Buffett is quoted as saying "The most important investment you can make is in yourself."

---

1. Energy Levels: Physical health directly affects energy levels. Regular exercise and a healthy diet contribute to better stamina and sustained energy throughout the day. Individuals with good physical health are often more alert and focused, which can enhance their productivity at work.

2. Cognitive Function: Physical activity has been linked to improved cognitive function. Regular exercise increases blood flow to the brain and promotes the growth of new neurons, which can enhance memory, learning, and decision-making. These cognitive benefits can positively influence work-related tasks and problem-solving.

3. Physical activity is a natural stress reliever. Engaging in regular exercise helps reduce levels of stress hormones, such as cortisol and stimulates the production of endorphins, which are known as "feel-good" hormones. Managing stress is crucial for maintaining focus and efficiency at work.

4. Improved Sleep: Physical activity and good overall health contribute to better sleep quality. Quality sleep is essential for cognitive function, mood regulation, and overall well-being. Employees who prioritize their physical health are more likely to experience restful sleep, which can positively impact their work performance.

5. Reduced Absenteeism: Individuals with better physical health are less prone to illness and are, therefore, less likely to miss work due to health-related issues. This can result in increased attendance and consistent productivity.

6. Enhanced Resilience: Good physical health can enhance an individual's resilience to workplace stressors. Resilient employees are better equipped to handle challenges, bounce back from setbacks, and maintain a positive attitude, all of which contribute to sustained work efficiency.

7. Team Dynamics: Physical health also can impact team dynamics. Employees who prioritize their health may be more engaged, collaborative, and supportive of their colleagues. A healthy and positive workplace culture can foster a more productive and efficient work environment.

8. Prevention of Chronic Diseases: Maintaining physical health through regular exercise and a balanced diet can help prevent chronic diseases, such as cardiovascular conditions, diabetes, and obesity. Prevention of these health issues can contribute to long-term work efficiency by reducing the impact of health-related challenges.

Employers are increasingly recognizing the importance of promoting employee well-being, including physical health, as part of their overall strategy to enhance productivity and job satisfaction. Many workplace wellness programs now focus on encouraging healthy lifestyle choices to benefit both employees and the organization.

Quick workouts and desk exercises are great for maintaining physical activity, especially if you have a sedentary job. You may have not considered this, but here are some exercises you can incorporate into your "work at your desk" routine:

Quick exercises you can do at your desk:

1. Seated Leg Lifts:

    *   Sit straight in your chair and lift one leg off the ground, straightening it. Hold for a few seconds, then lower it without letting it touch the floor. Repeat on the other leg.

2. Chair Dips:

    *   Sit on the edge of your chair with your hands gripping the edge. Slide off the chair and lower your body by bending your elbows. Push back up.

3. Desk Push-Ups:

    *   Stand a couple of feet away from your desk. Place your hands on the edge of the desk shoulder-width apart. Lean forward and do push-ups against the desk.

4. Chair Squats:

    *   Stand in front of your chair. Lower your body as if you were sitting down, then stand back up. Repeat for 15–20 reps.

5. Desk Planks:

    - Place your hands on your desk, shoulder-width apart. Step back until your body is in a straight line, and hold the plank position for 30–60 seconds.

6. Calf Raises:

    - Stand behind your chair and rise up onto your toes, lifting your heels off the ground. Lower your heels back down. Repeat for 15–20 reps.

7. March in Place:

    - Lift your knees high while marching in place for 1–2 minutes. This is a great way to get your heart rate up without leaving your desk.

Remember to take short breaks throughout the day to stretch and move around. These quick exercises can help you stay active and reduce the negative effects of prolonged sitting. Your co-workers will wonder what you are doing but stick with it. It makes you unique and interesting

Work Environment

We also need to operate in an environment that is conducive to doing our best work. Some of the environmental areas that can be impacted are length of commute, office, boss, team members, office environment, work from home, travel, etc.

Creating a conducive work environment is crucial for maximizing productivity and well-being. Here are some suggestions for optimizing the various aspects of your environment:

1. Length of Commute:

    - If possible, explore flexible work hours to avoid peak commute times.

    - Consider alternative transportation methods or remote work options to reduce commute stress.

2. Office:

    - Advocate for a well-designed and comfortable office space.

    - Collaborate with colleagues on office layout and design for better functionality.

3. Boss:

    - You probably can't change who your boss is, so foster open communication with your supervisor.

    - Discuss expectations, goals, and any challenges you may be facing in your role.

4. Team Members:

    - Foster a positive team culture by encouraging open communication and collaboration.

- Organize team-building activities to strengthen relationships.

5. Office Environment:

   - Advocate for a clean, organized, and ergonomic workspace.

   - Promote a positive office culture with a focus on teamwork and shared goals.

6. If You Work From Home:

   - Ensure you have the necessary tools and equipment for remote work.

   - Establish regular check-ins with colleagues to maintain a sense of connection.

7. Home Life:

   - Establish a dedicated workspace at home to separate work and personal life.

   - Set boundaries with family members to minimize interruptions during work hours.

8. Travel:

   - If travel is a significant aspect of your job, plan and organize trips efficiently.

   - Utilize technology for virtual meetings to minimize the need for frequent travel.

   - Create a daily schedule to balance work and personal responsibilities.

Not all changes need to be drastic. Small adjustments in any of these areas can cumulatively contribute to a more conducive work environment. Regularly reassess and adapt, based on your evolving needs and circumstances. And remember, the reason we are doing all this is so we can carve out a little time from our lunch hour to invest in our own career self-development.

Job Skills

Perhaps the most obvious ways we can use our lunch hour time is to increase personal and professional skills. This could include education, computer skills, reading, writing / spelling, arithmetic, technical knowledge, etc. Here are some resources for utilizing your lunch hour to increase skills:

Online Classes Can Help

There are a variety of platforms like:

1. Coursera, which offers unlimited access to 7,000+ world-class courses, hands-on projects, and job-ready certificate programs—all included in your subscription. Check out coursera.org, it is impressive what they offer.

2. Udemy – udemy.com. Learn confidently with up-to-date courses covering in-demand topics, such as development, data science, IT certification, web design, digital

marketing, leadership, communication, and more. Another impressive website with lots of educational options.

3. Khan Academy offers practice exercises, instructional videos, and a personalized learning dashboard that empowers learners to study at their own pace outside of the classroom. They tackle math, science, computing, history, art history, economics, and more, including K-14. They focus on skill mastery to help learners establish strong foundations, so there's no limit to what they can learn next! https://www.khanacademy.org/ is an impressive educational offering.

Skill Development Websites

1. Skillshare is an online learning community with thousands of classes for creative and curious people, on topics including illustration, design, photography, video, freelancing, and more. On Skillshare.com, you'll find inspiration from hands-on classes and teachers at the top of their creative fields, so you can take the next step in your creative journey.

2. LinkedIn Learning: Wikipedia says this is an American online learning platform that provides video courses taught by industry experts in software, creative endeavors, and

business skills. It is a subsidiary of LinkedIn. All the courses on LinkedIn fall into four categories: business, creative, technology, and certifications. https://learning.linkedin.com/ "Discover relevant e-learning content personalized to the needs of each learner, including content from our own world-class library of over 16,000 expertly produced online and consistently updated courses across seven languages."

3. YouTube University: "YouTube University" is a colloquial term used to describe the idea of learning through online videos and educational content available on YouTube. It is not an official institution or university but rather a metaphorical way of highlighting the diverse range of educational material that can be found on the YouTube platform. YouTube has become a vast repository of videos covering a wide array of subjects, including tutorials, lectures, educational channels, and informational content. Users can find content ranging from academic topics like mathematics, science, and history to practical skills such as programming, cooking, and language learning. Key features of "YouTube University" include:

    • Diversity of Content: YouTube offers content created by individuals, educators, professionals, and organizations worldwide. This diverse range of creators contributes to a rich and varied collection of educational material.

- Accessibility: Educational content on YouTube is often free and accessible to anyone with an internet connection. This democratizes learning by providing a platform from which individuals can access information and tutorials on a vast array of topics.

- Self-Paced Learning: Users can learn at their own pace by watching videos and tutorials whenever and wherever it is convenient for them. This flexibility is particularly valuable for individuals with varying schedules and commitments.

- Visual Learning: Many people find visual content more engaging and easier to understand. YouTube videos often include visual aids, demonstrations, and graphics, enhancing the learning experience.

- Community Engagement: YouTube allows for community interaction through comments, discussions, and collaborations. Viewers can engage with creators, ask questions, and participate in a virtual learning community.

While "YouTube University" can be a valuable resource for learning, it's important to note that not all content on the platform is accurate or reliable. Users should exercise discernment, verify information when needed, and seek content from reputable sources.

Formal education from accredited institutions is still crucial for certain professions and fields that require official certifications or degrees. However, for informal learning, skill-building, and gaining knowledge on a wide range of topics, YouTube can be a powerful and accessible tool.

I use YouTube whenever I need to repair something at home. For example, I recently bought a new microwave, and the salesperson said it was complicated to install and offered me a $150 installation option. I watched a YouTube video of a microwave like mine being installed, including all the information I needed to know for the job, and realized I could do this, no problem! It was not complicated, so I did the installation myself, saving $150.

Another example where YouTube was helpful is when I broke a taillight on my SUV, and the repair shop wanted $800 to replace it. YouTube showed me that I could buy the new taillight directly from the manufacturer for much less money. I also saw that it was a more difficult installation than I wanted to tackle, and it required special tools. So, I purchased the taillight online and went to another repair shop with my taillight in hand and they installed it for $100. Being an educated consumer can save you $$$.

Writing / Spelling Improvement

Writing and spelling are essential to job advancement. If you didn't learn these skills well in high school, it is not too late to bring these up to speed. You won't get far in most jobs unless you have good basic mastery of writing and spelling. Don't despair, computers can now do most of this for us!

a) Writing: If you need it, dedicate time to improving your writing skills. Improving your writing and spelling skills takes practice, dedication, and a systematic approach. The best tip to improving your writing and spelling abilities is to learn how to use the tools that come with your computer and the word processing program you use. Mine checks spelling and grammar, and my content is much improved.

b) Write Every Day: Set aside time at lunch each day to write. Practice is essential for improvement. Write about different topics, experiment with different styles, and challenge yourself with various forms of writing (e.g., essays, short stories, blog posts).

c) Read Regularly: Expose yourself to a variety of written materials, including books, articles, and essays. This will help you absorb different writing styles, expand your vocabulary, and improve your overall language skills. I recommend you do your reading on Libby. It is free and very user friendly.

d) Seek Feedback: Share your writing with others, and ask for constructive feedback. Whether it's from peers, teachers, or online communities, getting input from others can provide valuable insights and help you identify areas for improvement. My boss's secretary liked me and was willing to give me constructive feedback.

e) If All Else Fails, Take a Writing Course: Consider enrolling in writing courses, either online or in-person. Many platforms offer courses on grammar, style, and creative writing. Workshops and classes can provide structured learning and opportunities for feedback.

f) Expand Your Vocabulary: Learn new words regularly and try to incorporate them into your writing. Play vocabulary games on your smartphone during your lunch hour. Several popular smartphone games are designed to enhance vocabulary skills while providing an entertaining and engaging experience. Playing these games is not goofing off if you are doing it to improve a necessary skill. And the fact that it is fun is an added free bonus for you.

Here are some well-known games that can help improve your vocabulary:

1. Wordscapes is a word puzzle game in which players are presented with a set of letters, and must arrange them to form words that fit into a crossword-style grid. I love this one!

2. Scrabble GO is a mobile version of the classic Scrabble game. Players use letter tiles to create words on a game board, competing against friends or AI opponents. It's an excellent way to expand your vocabulary while enjoying a classic word game.

3. Elevate is more than just a vocabulary game; it's a comprehensive brain training app. It offers activities to improve various cognitive skills, including reading, writing, listening, and speaking. The vocabulary-building exercises are designed to enhance your overall language proficiency.

4. QuizUp is a trivia game that covers a wide range of topics, including vocabulary and word games. You can compete against friends or other players in real-time quizzes, testing your knowledge in various categories.

5. 7 Little Words is a unique word puzzle game that challenges players to find the seven words associated with a particular clue. The

game offers a daily puzzle, and each puzzle provides an opportunity to discover new words. I like this one.

6. Word Cookies is a word puzzle game in which players swipe to connect letters and form words. It offers a variety of levels with increasing difficulty, making it a fun way to challenge and expand your vocabulary.

7. Crossword Puzzle Redstone: This crossword puzzle app provides daily crossword challenges of varying difficulty levels. Solving crosswords is an excellent way to encounter new words and reinforce existing vocabulary.

Remember that while these games can be enjoyable and beneficial for vocabulary improvement, they are just one component of language development. Combining these games with reading books, articles, and engaging in conversations will contribute to a well-rounded enhancement of your vocabulary skills.

Improvement takes time, so be patient with yourself. Consistent effort and a willingness to learn from mistakes will contribute significantly to your progress. When you have the time, use it wisely. Remember what Nelson Mandela said: "It always seems impossible until it's done."

Arithmetic and Math Skills

Never say aloud that you are no good at math! Expressing a belief that you are not good at math (or remembering names, etc.) out loud can indeed contribute to a self-fulfilling prophecy, and may have a broader impact on both you and those around you. Here are a few reasons why verbalizing a negative perception of your math abilities can be detrimental:

1. Self-Fulfilling Prophecy: As mentioned earlier, verbalizing a negative belief about your math skills can influence your behavior and performance. If you consistently tell yourself and others that you are not good at math, you may inadvertently limit your efforts to improve and reinforce a negative mindset.

2. Impact on Confidence and Motivation: Expressing a lack of proficiency in math can erode your confidence and motivation to tackle math-related challenges. Confidence is a key factor in learning and problem-solving, and a negative mindset can hinder your ability to approach mathematical problems with a proactive and open mindset.

3. Influence on Others: Verbalizing your perceived shortcomings in math can influence those around you, particularly peers and younger individuals. It may

inadvertently reinforce stereotypes or create a perception that certain individuals are inherently not good at math. This can be damaging, especially in educational or professional settings in which collaboration and support are essential.

4. Difficulty Overcoming Preconceived Notions: Once a negative belief is planted, it can be challenging to overcome, even if there is improvement. Others may continue to associate you with the initial perception, making it harder to change their opinions or your own self-perception, even when progress is made.

To counteract these negative effects, it's important to adopt a growth mindset and focus on the idea that skills, including math proficiency, can be developed through effort and dedication. Encouraging positive self-talk and reframing challenges as opportunities for growth can contribute to a more constructive and open approach to learning and improving in math.

Remember, your smartphone and computer can do any kind of math you need. You just need to learn how to use them. Here are some ways to improve your math skills.

•   Try Photo Math: Photomath is a mobile app owned by Google. It is a computer algebra system with an augmented optical character recognition system designed for use with a smartphone's camera to scan and recognize mathematical equations; the app then displays step-by-step explanations onscreen. It's somewhat like using Google Translate when you are communicating with people in a foreign country who don't speak your language.

- If you have Excel on your computer, go to "Formulas," then select "Insert Function," and in the "Search for a Function" box, type a brief description of what you want to do and click "Go." It performs amazing math!

There are many other math training programs on the Web. For example:

- IXL Math — Features: IXL offers a personalized learning experience with practice problems for various math concepts. It covers topics from pre-K to calculus, and provides instant feedback to help you understand and correct mistakes.

- Wolfram Alpha — Features: Wolfram Alpha is a powerful computational engine that can help you solve math problems step-by-step. It's especially useful for checking your work and understanding the process behind mathematical solutions.

- Brilliant — Features: Brilliant offers interactive learning in math and science. It focuses on problem-solving and critical thinking, making it an engaging platform to improve your math skills. It covers a wide range of topics from basic to advanced.

- Purplemath — Features: Purplemath provides free resources and lessons on algebra, covering topics like linear equations, inequalities, and factoring. The explanations are clear, making it a valuable resource for self-study.

- Paul's Online Math Notes — Features: This resource offers comprehensive tutorials and notes on a variety of math topics, from algebra to calculus. It's a great supplement to your learning, providing detailed explanations and examples.

- GeoGebra — Features: GeoGebra is a dynamic mathematics software that brings together geometry, algebra, spreadsheets, graphing, and more. It's a versatile tool for visualizing and exploring mathematical concepts.

To gain more self confidence in your math skills, Khan Academy offers comprehensive lessons on a wide range of math topics, starting from basic arithmetic to advanced calculus. The lessons are presented through video tutorials and practice exercises.

Remember to practice consistently, and don't hesitate to revisit fundamental concepts to build a strong foundation. Whether you prefer interactive apps, video lessons, or written tutorials, there are plenty of resources available to suit your learning style.

Staying Up to Date on Industry Trends

Make it a habit to allocate time regularly for staying updated. By diversifying your sources and using a combination of these strategies, you can build and maintain a comprehensive understanding of the latest developments in your industry.

1. Utilize Social Media:

    - Follow relevant accounts, companies, and influencers on social media platforms, such as X (formerly Twitter) and LinkedIn. These platforms often provide real-time updates on industry news, events, and discussions. However, if you are not careful you could end up spending a lot of unproductive time on these!

2. Join Online Forums and Communities:

    - Participate in online forums and communities related to your industry. Platforms like Reddit, Stack Overflow, or specialized industry forums provide a space for professionals to discuss trends, share knowledge, and seek advice.

3. Attend Webinars and Virtual Events:

    •   Many organizations host webinars, virtual conferences, and online events. Participate in these to gain insights from industry experts, learn about new technologies, and network with professionals in your field.

4. Read Industry Publications:

    •   Subscribe to or regularly check industry publications, magazines, and journals. These sources often feature in-depth articles, case studies, and analyses of current trends and technologies.

5. Podcasts:

    •   Listen to industry-specific podcasts. Many podcasts feature interviews with experts, discussions on current trends, and insights into emerging technologies.

6. Set Google Alerts:

    •   Set up Google Alerts for relevant keywords related to your industry. Google will send you email notifications when new content matching your chosen keywords is published.

7. Follow Company Blogs and Updates:

    •   Stay informed about updates from companies that are leaders in your industry. Many technology companies have blogs or news sections on their websites where they share updates, product releases, and insights.

Mindfulness

By now, all this information may be causing you some stress. Here are some ideas for mindfulness that can help reduce your stress.

- Mindful Breathing: Find a quiet and comfortable space. Sit or lie down in a relaxed position. Close your eyes and focus your attention on your breath. Inhale slowly through your nose, feeling your lungs expand. Exhale slowly through your mouth, releasing any tension. Repeat this process, bringing your mind back to your breath if it wanders.

- Mindful Walking: Take a short walk, paying attention to each step and the sensations in your body. Focus on the sights, sounds, and smells around you. If your mind starts to wander, gently bring it back to the present moment.

- Nature Connection: Spend time in nature, whether it's a park, garden, or a nearby natural setting. Observe the beauty around you, listen to the sounds of nature, and take deep breaths.

- Create a Routine: Incorporate mindfulness activities into your daily routine. Set aside dedicated time, even if it's just a few minutes each day, to practice mindfulness.

Remember, mindfulness is a skill that develops with practice. Start with small steps, be patient with yourself, and gradually increase the duration or complexity of your mindfulness activities. Consistency is key to experiencing the long-term benefits of these practices.

Develop a Positive Mental Attitude

Developing a positive mental attitude is a challenging task, but there are actions you can take to enhance this aspect of your life. Your personality, sense of humor, positive interactions with others, social skills, and engaging in fun activities that enrich your life can collectively make you a more employable person. Developing a positive mental attitude is indeed a valuable and rewarding endeavor. Here are practical steps you can take to enhance your mental attitude:

1. Practice Gratitude:

   - Take time each day to reflect on things you're grateful for.

   - Keep a gratitude journal to note positive experiences, achievements, or people you appreciate.

2. Positive Affirmations:

    • Create positive affirmations that reflect your strengths and goals.

    • Repeat these affirmations regularly to reinforce a positive self-image.

3. Surround Yourself With Positivity:

    • Spend time with positive and supportive people.

    • Distance yourself from negativity and toxic relationships.

4. Adopt a Sense of Humor:

    • Cultivate a sense of humor and find reasons to laugh daily.

    • Learn to see the lighter side of situations.

5. Set Realistic Goals:

    • Break down larger goals into smaller, achievable tasks.

    • Celebrate your successes, no matter how small, to build a sense of accomplishment.

6. Focus on Solutions:

    • When faced with challenges, focus on finding solutions rather than dwelling on problems.

    • Develop a problem-solving mindset

and approach obstacles with a positive attitude.

7. Mindfulness and Presence:

- Avoid dwelling on the past or worrying excessively about the future.

8. Self-Care:

- Prioritize self-care activities that contribute to your well-being.

- Ensure you get enough sleep, exercise regularly, and maintain a healthy diet.

9. Continuous Learning:

- Embrace a growth mindset by viewing challenges as opportunities to learn and grow.

- Engage in continuous learning to expand your knowledge and skills.

10. Kindness and Empathy:

- Practice kindness towards yourself and others.

- Cultivate empathy to better understand and connect with people.

11. Positive Interactions:

- Foster positive interactions with colleagues, friends, and family.

- Be a good listener, express genuine interest, and offer support when needed.

12. Engage in Hobbies:

    - Pursue activities that bring you joy and fulfillment.

    - Set aside time for hobbies and interests outside of work.

13. Volunteer or Help Others:

    - Contributing to the well-being of others can provide a sense of purpose and fulfillment.

    - Volunteer for causes that resonate with you.

14. Reflect on Successes:

    - Regularly reflect on your achievements and positive experiences.

    - Use past successes as motivation for future endeavors.

15. Limit Negative Influences:

    - Be mindful of the news media and content you consume.

    - Limit exposure to negative news and focus on uplifting and inspiring material.

16. Seek Professional Support:

    - If necessary, consider seeking the guidance of a mental health professional.

    - Therapy or counseling can provide tools

and strategies to maintain a positive mental attitude.

Remember, developing a positive mental attitude is an ongoing process. It requires self-awareness, commitment, and a willingness to cultivate habits that contribute to a more optimistic and resilient mindset.

Honest self-assessment is challenging, because we can't see ourselves as others see us, and people often hesitate to share the truth to avoid hurting our feelings. Hang in there, and opportunities will come to light as you continue to read.

Case Study: Alex's Positive Transformation

Consider Alex, who initially struggled with maintaining a positive mental attitude at work. Recognizing the importance of a positive outlook, Alex decided to work on enhancing his sense of humor and social skills. He started incorporating light-hearted moments into his interactions with colleagues, and engaged in team-building activities.

Over time, Alex observed a positive shift in his workplace dynamics. His improved social skills not only made him more approachable, but also resulted in stronger connections with his co-workers. This positive change contributed to a more enjoyable and collaborative work environment.

Although it took some time and effort, Alex's commitment to fostering a positive mental attitude eventually paid off. His case serves as a tangible example of how personal development in areas like personality and social skills can lead to a more fulfilling and employable professional life.

1. Humor in the Workplace:

    - Before: Alex used to approach work with a serious demeanor, rarely injecting humor into his interactions.

    - Transformation: Recognizing the power of humor, Alex started incorporating light jokes and positive banter into his daily conversations with colleagues.

    - Outcome: The workplace atmosphere lightened up, and colleagues began to appreciate Alex's positive energy. Meetings became more engaging, fostering a more enjoyable work environment.

2. Enhanced Social Skills:

    - Before: Alex was somewhat reserved and hesitant to initiate conversations with his peers.

    - Transformation: Alex actively worked on his social skills by attending team-building events, initiating small talk during breaks, and participating in group activities.

- Outcome: Alex's improved social skills led to stronger connections with colleagues. He became more approachable, and his willingness to collaborate with others was noticed, contributing to a more cohesive and cooperative team.

3. Increased Team Collaboration:

   - Before: Alex often worked independently, not actively seeking input or collaboration from others.

   - Transformation: Realizing the benefits of teamwork, Alex started involving his colleagues in projects, seeking their opinions, and providing constructive feedback.

   - Outcome: The increased collaboration resulted in more innovative solutions, and Alex's projects began to stand out. This positive change not only enhanced his professional reputation, but also opened up new opportunities for growth within the organization.

4. Positive Work Relationships:

   - Before: Alex's work relationships were cordial but lacked depth.

   - Transformation: By fostering a positive mental attitude, Alex began actively nurturing work relationships. He

started acknowledging colleagues'
accomplishments, offering support
during challenging times, and
expressing gratitude.

- Outcome: Colleagues responded
  positively to Alex's genuine interest
  in their well-being, creating a more
  supportive and encouraging work
  environment. This not only improved
  morale, but also contributed to
  increased job satisfaction among the
  team.

In summary, Alex's intentional efforts to enhance his personality and social skills resulted in a more fulfilling and employable professional life for Alex. The incorporation of humor, improved social interactions, increased collaboration, and positive work relationships, collectively contributed to Alex being more approachable and therefore being included in more opportunities to contribute. All this adds up to Alex being a more valuable employee, and everything he learned he gets to take with him should he ever feel the need to leave this company.

I just hit you with a whole lot of theory, take what works, and toss the rest. My goal is to get you thinking about possibilities. You can't do it all, but you can tackle some of the ideas that will make a difference in the overall success of your turbocharge endeavor.

Chapter 10 – The Bottom Line

"The only thing standing between you and your goal is the story you keep telling yourself as to why you can't achieve it." — Jordan Belfort

"The only limits that exist are the ones you place on yourself." — Dr. Wayne Dyer

You Must Learn to be Self-Disciplined

We have established that your lunch hour belongs to you. We have proven that it is a fact that during your career, you may have as much as four years of time you can use to do fun and productive things that can help turbocharge your career in the long run. But nothing good will come of this, unless you hold yourself accountable.

The best way to hold yourself accountable is to make a lunchtime to-do list and then cross items off as they get done. Making the list is the easy part, actually doing the items on your list takes self-discipline. But a list is the best way to start. If it is on paper (or on your smartphone, or in your computer) there is a much higher chance that you will actually do it someday.

Developing self-discipline is a gradual process that involves cultivating positive habits and a mindset. Here are some strategies to help you become more self-disciplined:

1. Set Clear Goals:

   - Define specific, measurable, achievable, relevant, and time-bound (SMART) goals. Having a clear vision of what you want to achieve will give you direction.

2. Prioritize Tasks:

   - Identify your most important tasks and

prioritize them. Focus on high-priority activities that align with your goals before tackling less critical ones.

3. Create a Schedule:

    •   Develop a daily or weekly schedule. Allocate specific time blocks for different tasks, including work, breaks, and personal activities. Stick to your schedule as much as possible.

4. Break Tasks Into Smaller Steps:

    •   Large tasks can be overwhelming. Break them into smaller, more manageable steps. This makes it easier to stay focused and track your progress.

5. Remove Distractions:

    •   Identify and eliminate or minimize distractions. This might include turning off notifications, creating a designated workspace, or establishing specific time periods for focused work.

6. Build Habits:

    •   Habits are powerful tools for self-discipline. Start with small, consistent actions and gradually build them into routines. Over time, these routines will become habits that require less conscious effort.

7. Stay Consistent:

   - Consistency is key to developing discipline. Stick to your schedule and commitments, even when you don't feel like it. The more consistent you are, the more disciplined you become.

8. Learn to Say No:

   - Avoid overcommitting yourself. Learn to say no to tasks and activities that don't align with your priorities. This helps you stay focused on what truly matters.

9. Reward Yourself:

   - Celebrate your achievements, no matter how small. Set up a system of rewards for reaching milestones, and use these rewards to motivate yourself.

10. Stay Positive and Mindful:

    - Cultivate a positive mindset. Focus on the benefits of your efforts rather than dwelling on potential challenges. Practice mindfulness to stay present and avoid getting overwhelmed by future tasks.

    - Take time to reflect on your progress. Assess what is working well and what needs improvement. Adjust your strategies accordingly.

11. Seek Support:

    - Share your goals with friends, family, or colleagues who can offer support and encouragement. Having a support system can help you stay accountable.

Remember, developing self-discipline is a gradual process, and setbacks are a normal part of the journey. Be patient with yourself and make adjustments as needed. Consistent effort over time will contribute to significant improvements in your self-discipline.

Instant Gratification vs. Greater Achievement

In a world that often celebrates instant gratification, there is a profound wisdom in embracing the principles of delayed achievement. The choice between seeking immediate rewards and adopting a slow-and-steady approach can significantly impact one's career achievements and, therefore, your financial success in the long run. Read on as we explore the benefits of patient, persistent efforts versus the allure of wanting everything now, supported by two case studies illustrating contrasting paths to financial prosperity.

The Slow and Steady Approach

- Education and Skill Development: Patience is a virtue in skill development and education. Individuals who invest time in acquiring valuable skills or pursuing advanced education tend to command higher salaries in the long term. This patient approach not only enhances earning potential but also fosters a sustainable and fulfilling career.

- Just like the slow and steady approach applies to your lunchtime career enhancement activities, the same approach applies to your financial life. Success involves disciplined savings and strategic investments. Individuals who prioritize saving a portion of their income consistently over time accumulate a substantial nest egg. This approach enables the power of compounding, in which the interest earned on savings generates additional returns, contributing to long-term financial growth.

- Building a Diversified Investment Portfolio: Slow and steady financial success involves a methodical approach to investments. Diversifying one's investment portfolio over various asset classes, such as stocks, bonds, and real estate, mitigates risks and fosters stability. Over time, this diversified strategy often outperforms impulsive, high-risk investments.

The Instant Gratification Dilemma

- Impulsive Spending and Debt Accumulation: Those inclined towards instant gratification may succumb to impulsive spending habits, leading to the accumulation of debt. Credit card usage without a disciplined repayment strategy can result in high-interest payments, hindering financial stability and limiting opportunities for long-term wealth accumulation.

- Short-Term Gains, Long-Term Risks: The pursuit of quick financial gains, often associated with speculative investments or get-rich-quick schemes, poses substantial risks. Individuals seeking rapid returns may expose themselves to the volatility of markets, leading to significant financial setbacks in the long term.

- Limited Focus on Skill Development: Opting for immediate rewards might lead to a lack of focus on skill development or education. While quick gains may provide temporary satisfaction, the absence of a solid foundation in skills and knowledge can hinder sustained career growth and financial success.

Case Studies

1. John — The Patient Investor: John, an individual committed to a slow-and-steady financial approach, consistently saved a portion of his income and invested in a diversified portfolio. Over several decades, the power of compounding significantly grew his wealth. His patience in avoiding impulsive decisions and focusing on long-term goals resulted in financial security and a comfortable retirement.

2. Sarah — The Impulsive Spender: Sarah, driven by the desire for instant gratification, frequently made impulsive purchases and invested in high-risk ventures. While she experienced occasional windfalls, her lack of financial discipline and high levels of debt ultimately led to financial instability. Sarah's short-term gains proved unsustainable, highlighting the risks associated with instant gratification.

Conclusion: The choice between instant gratification and delayed achievement is a pivotal factor in determining long-term financial success. While the allure of immediate rewards may be tempting, embracing patience, consistent effort, and strategic planning often leads to a more secure and prosperous financial future. The case studies of John and Sarah exemplify the contrasting outcomes of these approaches, emphasizing the enduring value of slow and steady financial strategies.

You May Have 10 Jobs Before Retirement

As previously stated, according to the Bureau of Labor Statistics, the average worker currently holds 10 different jobs before age 48. I am not sure if they are talking about jobs you take to get by on, or jobs that are part of your overall career. For example, I worked at a temp job for four months performing claim adjusting work, but this was just to fill in the time after I got laid off until I found a better job with another company that I could learn and grow with. It seems the days of leaving school and going to work for a company, staying there until you retire, are mostly gone. There is definitely a trend of people having multiple career jobs before they retire. This trend makes it even more important that you use your precious reclaimed lunch hours to learn and tune up the skills that your next company is going to want. You don't need to be disloyal to your current company, but you do need to look out for yourself and your future.

Sometimes you must leave your current company to accomplish your long-term goals. You may be fully qualified for that newly opened position, but the company goes and hires an outsider that you are then asked to train. Once you get over your fear of the uncertainty of having a regular paycheck, you need to be that outsider that the next company in your career will hire. Only you know what skills you need to make this happen, but I am convinced that you can better prepare yourself by thoughtfully using some of your lunch hours.

Get Control of Your Personal Finances

This is a good time to suggest that you read a book on budgeting and financial planning, so that you can prepare for bigger and better jobs. It is important that you have the financial backing to make the leap, if necessary. Being financially ready to change jobs will help you navigate the transition period with greater ease and peace of mind. Following are some key steps to ensure financial preparedness, if you find the need for a job change.

1. Assess Your Current Financial Situation:

   - Review your current financial status, including savings, investments, debts, and monthly expenses. Understanding your financial baseline is crucial for making informed decisions.

2. Create a Budget:

   - Develop a detailed budget that outlines your essential expenses (e.g., rent or mortgage, utilities, groceries) and discretionary spending. Identify areas where you can cut back if needed.

   - Consider using Ramsey Solutions EveryDollar budgeting software. They have a free version that is fantastic. It will help you get your finances organized, make a plan, build up your confidence, and kick money stress out of your life for good.

3. Emergency Fund:

   • Ensure you have an emergency fund with three to six months' worth of living expenses. This fund serves as a financial safety net in case of unexpected expenses or a temporary period without income. This may sound like pie in the sky, but many people do this, and so can you.

4. Evaluate Benefits and Retirement Savings:

   • Consider the impact of changing jobs on your benefits, including health insurance and retirement plans. Understand the benefits offered by potential employers and factor these into your decision.

By taking these steps, you can position yourself for financial success during a job change and mitigate potential challenges that may arise during the transition. Everyone's financial situation is unique, so it's important to tailor these steps to your specific circumstances and goals.

I personally have followed the 10-10-80 rule for a long time. It has served me well. The 10-10-80 approach to long-term financial success is a simple yet effective financial management strategy that emphasizes disciplined allocation of income to different areas of life. This approach encourages individuals to allocate 10% of their income to charitable giving, another 10% to savings or investments, and to live on the remaining 80%. This balanced approach aims to foster financial stability, build wealth, and contribute to the well-being of both the individual and the community.

1. 10% to Charity:

    - Purpose: Encourages a sense of social responsibility and giving back to the community.

    - Benefits:

        o Personal Fulfillment: Contributing to charitable causes provides a sense of purpose and personal fulfillment.
        o Community Impact: Supporting charitable organizations helps address societal needs and creates positive change.

2. 10% to Savings or Investments:

    - Purpose: Builds a financial safety net and lays the foundation for future wealth creation.

    - Benefits:

        o Emergency Fund: Establishing savings ensures financial security during unexpected events or emergencies.

- o Wealth Accumulation: Regular investments contribute to long-term wealth growth through compounding.

3. Live on 80%:

- Purpose: Promotes responsible spending and lifestyle choices within one's means.

- Benefits:

  - o Debt Avoidance: Living within 80% of income helps avoid accumulating unnecessary debt.
  - o Financial Discipline: Encourages budgeting and financial discipline, preventing overspending.

4. Key Principles:

- Discipline: The 10-10-80 approach requires consistent discipline in adhering to the allocated percentages.

- Long-Term Focus: Emphasizes the importance of long-term financial planning and sustainability.

- Flexibility: While the 10-10-80 guideline is a helpful framework, it allows for flexibility based on individual circumstances.

Case Study: Maria's Financial Journey:

- Charitable Giving: Maria allocates 10% of her income to various charitable causes, supporting local nonprofits and causes she is passionate about.

- Savings and Investments: Another 10% goes into her savings account and investments, ensuring she has an emergency fund and is building wealth over time. This is automatically deducted from her paycheck.

- Living Expenses: Maria has created a budget that allows her to live comfortably within 80% of her income, avoiding unnecessary debt and making mindful spending choices.

Conclusion:

The 10-10-80 approach serves as a practical guide for achieving long-term financial success by fostering a balanced financial lifestyle. It not only promotes individual well-being and financial security, but also encourages a positive impact on the community through charitable giving. This approach can be tailored to individual circumstances, providing a flexible, yet structured, framework for financial management.

Does Thinking About All This Stress You Out?

Managing stress is crucial for overall well-being, and can significantly improve your outcomes in various aspects of life. Here are some strategies to help you manage stress effectively:

1. Identify Stressors:

   - Recognize the sources of stress in your life. It could be work-related, personal, or a combination of factors.

   - Understand that some stressors are temporary, while others may be ongoing. Differentiating between the two can help you develop appropriate coping strategies.

2. Time Management:

   - Prioritize tasks and create a realistic schedule. Break down larger tasks into smaller, more manageable steps.

   - Learn to say no when necessary, and avoid overcommitting yourself.

3. Healthy Lifestyle:

   - Exercise regularly, as physical activity can help reduce stress hormones and trigger the release of endorphins, which are natural mood lifters.

- Maintain a balanced diet with nutritious foods, as certain nutrients can positively impact mood and energy levels.

4. Quality Sleep:

   - Establish a consistent sleep routine. Lack of sleep can exacerbate stress, while adequate rest can improve your ability to cope with challenges.

5. Mindfulness and Relaxation Techniques:

   - Practice mindfulness meditation, deep breathing, or progressive muscle relaxation to bring your focus to the present moment.

   - Engage in activities that promote relaxation, such as reading, listening to music, or taking a warm bath.

6. Social Support:

   - Share your thoughts and feelings with friends, family, or a trusted colleague. Talking about your stressors can provide a different perspective and emotional support.

   - Cultivate positive relationships, and spend time with people who uplift and support you.

7. Set Realistic Goals:

   - Break down your goals into achievable steps. Celebrate small victories along the way, and don't be too hard on yourself if things don't go as planned.

8. Positive Outlook:

   - Develop a positive mindset by focusing on what you can control rather than dwelling on things beyond your control.

   - Practice gratitude by acknowledging and appreciating the positive aspects of your life.

9. Learn to Delegate:

   - Delegate tasks when possible. Recognize that you don't have to do everything yourself, and seeking support is a sign of strength, not weakness.

> *"Never do for yourself what someone else can do for you better."* — Agatha Christie

10. Seek Professional Help:

    - If stress becomes overwhelming or persistent, consider seeking help from a mental health professional. A good therapist can provide coping strategies and support tailored to your specific situation.

Remember that managing stress is an ongoing process, and it's important to be patient with yourself as you incorporate these strategies into your daily life. Experiment with different techniques to find what works best for you, and be proactive in maintaining a healthy balance between work, personal life, and self-care.

People can experience stress in different ways and for different reasons. Some individuals may contribute to stressful situations, either intentionally or unintentionally, while others may find themselves in stressful circumstances due to external factors beyond their control.

Understanding and managing stress involves recognizing its sources, developing coping mechanisms, and fostering healthy communication and relationships. It's essential to approach stress from a holistic perspective, rather than attributing it solely to the actions of certain individuals. The bottom line is that stress management is a skill that individuals can cultivate to navigate life's challenges more effectively.

The Issue of Integrity

Former UCLA Basketball Coach John Wooden is supposed to have said: "The true test of a man's character is what he does when no one is watching."

The issue of integrity is critically important to your career advancement for several compelling reasons:

1. Professional Reputation: Integrity is the foundation of a strong professional reputation. Your colleagues, superiors,

and subordinates form opinions about you based on your ethical behavior. A reputation for honesty and integrity can enhance your credibility and trustworthiness in the workplace.

2. Trust and Relationships: Trust is a cornerstone of successful professional relationships. Colleagues, clients, and supervisors are more likely to rely on and collaborate with individuals they perceive as having high integrity. Building and maintaining trust contributes to effective teamwork and positive working relationships.

3. Career Advancement: Employers often value employees who consistently demonstrate integrity. Individuals with a strong sense of ethics are more likely to be considered for promotions and leadership roles. Employers seek individuals who can be trusted to make ethical decisions, especially in positions of greater responsibility.

4. Workplace Culture: A workplace with a culture of integrity is generally more positive and productive. Employees who prioritize ethical conduct contribute to a healthy work environment in which everyone is treated fairly and with respect. This, in turn, fosters collaboration and boosts overall morale.

5. Client and Customer Relationships: If your career involves interactions with clients or customers, integrity becomes even more crucial. Trust is a key factor in client relationships, and maintaining high ethical standards ensures that clients feel confident in your abilities and the services or products you provide.

6. Legal and Ethical Compliance: Many professions are subject to specific legal and ethical standards. Maintaining integrity ensures compliance with these standards, reducing the risk of legal issues or professional misconduct. Adhering to ethical guidelines helps you and your organization avoid legal and reputational consequences.

7. Personal Well-being: Having a strong sense of integrity contributes to your personal well-being. Knowing that you consistently act in an ethical manner can lead to greater job satisfaction and a sense of fulfillment in your career. Conversely, compromising your integrity can lead to stress, guilt, and potential long-term damage to your mental health.

8. Long-Term Success: While short-term gains might be possible through unethical behavior, long-term success often requires sustained integrity. A career built on a foundation of honesty and ethical conduct is

more likely to stand the test of time, leading to a sustainable and fulfilling professional journey.

In summary, integrity is not only a personal value, but a critical asset in the professional realm. It shapes your reputation, influences relationships, and contributes to a positive work environment. Prioritizing integrity in your career is an investment in long-term success and personal fulfillment.

Your Turn to Make a Plan

On the cover of this book, I claimed: **"10 simple things you can do on your lunch hour that will turbocharge your career!"** I gave you more than 10, but I am hoping you connected with at least 10 ideas that might work for you.

Circle of Continuous Improvement

Remember, in the journey of life, the Circle of Continuous Improvement stands as a powerful framework that propels individuals toward sustained growth and excellence. This circle is not just a concept; it is a mindset, a commitment to perpetual learning, and an unwavering belief in one's ability to evolve. This book challenged you into the realms of self-improvement, professional development, and the pursuit of our goals. Understanding and embracing this cycle becomes key to unlocking our full potential.

The first step in the Circle of Continuous Improvement is self-reflection. It's about taking a conscious pause to assess where you stand, acknowledging your strengths, identifying areas for development, and envisioning your aspirations. This introspective phase is not about self-criticism but rather a celebration of your journey so far, and a thoughtful consideration of where you want to go next. Write these down!

Once you have a clear understanding of your current position, the next step is to set meaningful and achievable goals. These goals act as your guiding stars, providing direction and purpose to your journey of improvement. Whether they are personal or professional, goals fuel motivation and create a roadmap for growth. Remember, each goal achieved becomes a stepping stone for the next level of accomplishment.

The heart of the Circle of Continuous Improvement lies in its emphasis on continuous learning. Life is an ever-evolving classroom, and each experience, success, or setback is an opportunity to gain valuable insights. Embrace a growth mindset, be open to new ideas, and be willing to adapt. As you accumulate knowledge and skills, apply them to enhance your capabilities and refine your approach.

A crucial component of the circle is taking decisive action. Your goals remain dreams until you translate them into tangible actions. Break down larger objectives into smaller, manageable tasks.

Consistent and purposeful action builds momentum, propelling you forward on your journey of improvement. Remember, it's not about perfection but about progress.

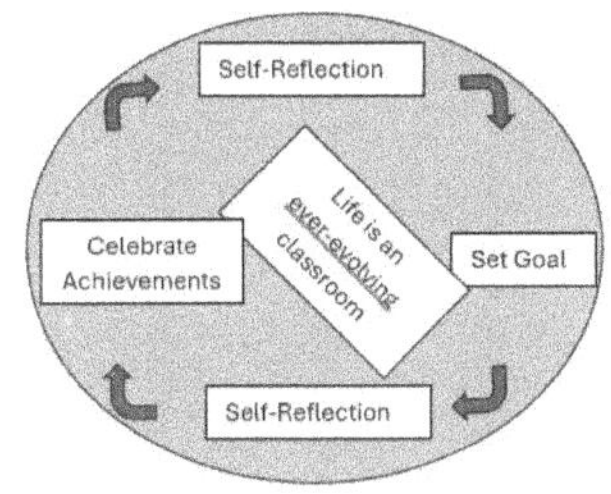

As you take action, the circle brings you back to reflection. Assess your progress, celebrate your achievements, and learn from your experiences. This cyclical process invites iteration—refining goals, adjusting strategies, and perpetuating the cycle of improvement. It's a dynamic, ever-renewing loop that keeps you engaged and committed to your personal and professional growth.

Several influential figures have shared wisdom on the importance of continuous improvement:

1. Winston Churchill: "To improve is to change; to be perfect is to change often."

2. Albert Einstein: "Life is like riding a bicycle. To keep your balance, you must keep moving."

Conclusion:

In adopting the Circle of Continuous Improvement, you embark on a transformative journey. It's not just about reaching a destination but about the joy of the journey itself. Embrace the process, savor the learning, and relish the growth. As you nurture this mindset, you'll find that improvement becomes not just a destination but a way of life, and success becomes a natural byproduct of your commitment to continuous growth. So, step into the circle, and let the cycle of improvement guide you to new heights of personal and professional excellence.

May I recommend that every January first of every year, you stop for a moment and celebrate what you've accomplished during the last year, and make a new list for the upcoming year.

I wish you much success and happiness!

Do You Have a Good Story to Add to This Book?

If you have an activity or story that helps prove the points I am making in this book, go to https://www.dandyce.com and I may include them in future versions of this book. Besides your story, please include:

Your name: ___________________________

Your email address: ___________________

Phone number: _______________________

May I call you? Yes   No

Do I have permission to put your idea or story in a future volume of this book? Yes   No

If you give me permission, and I use your story, do you want me to give you credit by name?
Yes   No

About the Author

Dan Dyce, CPCU RPA CTM is a consultant specializing in residential earthquake claim handling. His forte is the ability to train claim adjusters on earthquake policy coverage and claim handling in a humorous and memorable way. He is often called upon to teach the California Earthquake Claim Handling Accreditation class that adjusters who might handle an earthquake claim in California must take every three years.

For 14 years prior to 2015, he was the Claim Manager for the California Earthquake Authority (CEA), the largest residential earthquake insurance company in the USA. In that capacity, he oversaw the earthquake claim handling of 21 insurance companies that were responsible to take and process CEA earthquake claims.

He was previously a claim manager with CIGNA insurance company where he supervised commercial and residential property claims in seven Western states.

Dan served as a Consultant to the Applied Technology Council, and was a member of the Project Technical Committee for the update of the CUREE Guidelines for the assessment and repair of earthquake damage in residential woodframe buildings.

He served on the governing board for The California Residential Mitigation Program (CRMP). CRMP was established to assist California homeowners who wish to seismically retrofit their houses with grants and incentives.

Dan is a graduate of California State Polytechnic University, and has worked in the insurance industry his whole career. He has held positions in underwriting, insurance operations, and claims. He is a CPCU (Chartered Property and Casualty Underwriter) and a past president of Sacramento Valley Chapter of CPCU. He also has earned the RPA (Registered Professional Adjuster) designation. He earned a CTM from Toastmasters.

He has written articles for NU *Claims* as well as *Insights Journal*. He is a regular part of the earthquake coverage panel at the Annual Claims Conference for PLRB (Property Loss Research Bureau), and has presented at the CPCU Annual Meeting and Seminars.

Dan gives an entertaining and motivational keynote speech based on the concepts presented in this book. This talk can be tailored to the audience and time available. Contact him to schedule a presentation for your next conference.

https://www.dandyce.com

Keynote Speech Based on This Book

*Graphic from PLRB.org PLRB Presents

Dan Dyce presents an entertaining and motivational keynote speech based on this book. The cost is a speaking fee plus all travel costs.

If you would like him to present to your group, contact him at dandyce.com. Take a look at https://www.dandyce.com to get a preview of this speech.

If you like, you can purchase books in bulk numbers at wholesale prices to give to the attendees of this presentation. Or, Mr. Dyce can make books available for purchase at retail price in the back of the room after his presentation. He will autograph the books for anyone who wants it.

Appendix A

Some Easy Make-at-home Lunches:

1. My favorite, Turkey and Cheese — Sliced deli oven roasted turkey, any sliced cheese you like, fresh bread, spread mayo and mustard on the bread, add lettuce and or pickles. Put it in a plastic bag, add an apple and put it into a brown paper lunch bag. Yum!

2. Turkey Caesar Sandwich – Same turkey sandwich, but with Caesar dressing instead of mayo. It is best to assemble the sandwiches the day of, instead of the night before to avoid soggy sandwiches.

3. Tuna Salad Sandwich – Place drained tuna in a medium bowl. Add plain Greek yogurt (or mayonnaise), relish, red onion, celery, and a little salt and pepper. Stir with a fork until everything is well combined. Taste and add more salt and pepper as needed. Serve tuna salad on bread, rolls, croissants or crackers.

4. Egg Salad Sandwich – Make boiled eggs. Peel and mash the eggs with mayonnaise, add salt and pepper to taste. Add any of the following that you prefer: mustard, chopped green onion, sliced celery, sprinkle with dill.

Blend carefully and serve cold on bread, a salad, or in a wrap.

5. Arnold Palmer Sandwich – Half tuna, half egg salad.

6. Salami and Cream Cheese Sandwich — Spread mustard on one slice of bread; top with salami and arugula. Spread cream cheese on the other slice of bread; close sandwich. Serve, or refrigerate, wrapped tightly in wax paper or plastic, up to overnight.

7. Crisp Tuna-Cabbage Salad — Spread mustard on one slice of bread; top with tuna right out of the can and shredded cabbage. Spread cream cheese on the other slice of bread; close sandwich. Serve, or refrigerate, wrapped tightly in wax paper or plastic, up to overnight.

8. Chickpea Salad Sandwich – Start with a can of chickpeas, mash it up, gather a few slices of your favorite bread, some leafy greens, mash an avocado to spread if you like, and this is one great sandwich. Full of protein, fiber, texture and flavor.

Most of these can be put into a wrap if you like, but you get the idea. Fast, simple, healthy and saves money.